SECULARISATION

SECULARISATION

Edward Norman

New Century Theology

continuum
LONDON • NEW YORK

CONTINUUM

The Tower Building, 11 York Road, London SE1 7NX

370 Lexington Avenue, New York, NY 10017–6503

www.continuumbooks.com

First published 2002

Reprinted 2002

© 2002 Edward Norman

All rights reserved. No part of this publication may be reproduced or transmitted in any form or by any means, electronic or mechanical, including photocopying, recording or any information storage or retrieval system, without prior permission in writing from the publishers.

British Library Cataloguing-in-Publication Data

A catalogue record for this book is available from the British Library.

ISBN: 0-8264-5945-5

Typeset by Kenneth Burnley, Wirral, Cheshire

Printed in Great Britain by Biddles Ltd *www.biddles.co.uk*

Contents

Preface

The analysis which follows is not a systematic attempt – of the sort which might be made by a social scientist – to describe and identify every feature of a fading religious landscape. It is a landscape, indeed, which was once familiar, and yet which now appears in almost unrecognisable sequences to those who have lived within it all their lives. They, and many external observers, are saddened and perplexed by the decline of institutional religion in England, and cannot clearly discern the full nature of the causes. This study is not systematic in the sense that it does not try to assemble an exhaustive list of contributory conditions which may explain what is happening to the Church; what it does seek to do, however, is to account for a number of the fundamental transformations in religious understanding itself which try to help the reader to get something like a larger picture.

The view is generally one arranged from within the perspective of the national Church, the Church of England. This is partly because the Church's supposedly comprehensive nature – a legacy, in part, of its historical development, and also an impression based on its ideological incoherence – enables features of Anglicanism to describe the general condition. For very many English people, whose nominal adhesion to any faith is left distinctly – even joyously – imprecise, the Church of England is still how they understand Christianity to be. Even within the Roman Catholic

Church, with its greater uniformity of self-identity – as one would expect of a truly international body – the laity (and even a few clergy) are drifting into habits of thought, and views about the acceptance of religious authority, which share much common ground with the national Protestantism. The imagined comprehensiveness of Anglicanism has deceptive qualities. It is not very comprehensive in social terms, for example, being almost instantly recognisable as a social class phenomenon. Nor is its theology particularly comprehensive: it is incoherent, not incorporative; a kind of half-rejected digest of Calvinism made in the sixteenth and seventeenth centuries, and never really adjusted to match the surviving traditionalism of the Church's organisational structure. It has been in decline for an exceedingly long time, both in numerical support for its presence in society and in terms of its public vocation in the life of the nation.

'Decline' itself, like the concept of 'secularisation', is not entirely accurately employed to describe the state of religion. What is now perceived as decline has sometimes always been the case, and it is just that actual data, or screens of interpretation through which to discern its meaning, have been lacking in the past. Enthusiasm by the population for attendance at church services, now supposed to be at a particularly low level (and still receding fast), has never been especially marked, at any rate in the past couple of centuries. Secularisation is a subtle process, or accumulation of processes, which many regret but whose evidences they look upon helplessly. It is unquestionably very advanced in this society, yet it is always necessary to be mindful that decline of organised religion due to lost social habit, or to the impact of secularising ideas, does not necessarily mean that people are losing an inclination to seek personal identity through modules of understanding which they would probably call 'spiritual'. It may be that we are living through a time not of religious decline but of transformation in the understanding of religion. What does seem clear is that the public generally rather regrets the obviously receding influence of the Church and are unable to understand why it is occurring.

For it has happened due to lost habit, rather than any distinctive impact with discernably hostile ideology. Yet there is, as it happens, a deception here, too. The Church has indeed encountered hostile ideology but it has not, and nor has either the public or the intelligentsia, recognised it as such. Perhaps in a society like England, where precise theoretical analysis is not considered a necessary or a desired accompaniment of the conduct of public affairs, this was unavoidable. The reflections which follow suggest that the main reason for the velocity with which the Church is in decline derives from its own internal secularisation, from its voluntary and largely unconscious adoption of the ideas and practices of the benign adversaries who came to it with friendly countenances and largely innocent intentions. The book also suggests, therefore, that it is secular Humanism, as an unconscious orientation of life and thought, and entertained in an inarticulate and unrecognised form, which has with frightening frequency infiltrated the church members' perception of their own religion. Christianity is not being *rejected* in modern society – what is causing the decline of public support for the Church is the insistence of church leaders themselves in representing secular enthusiasm for humanity as core Christianity. In one sense, the Church now has little to declare that is distinctive in a society which is hard put to turn out for a football match, let alone a religious service. Institutional Christianity has lost the capacity to influence the culture on the one hand, and the culture is progressively secularised on the other.

The Church could, in another arrangement of things, have withstood the secularisation of the culture. It is not the general secularisation as such which has felled it, but the adoption by the Church of secular thought – death by one's own hand. At the time of my BBC Reith Lectures in 1978 I contended that secularisation at that time took the form of the *politicisation* of Christianity by its own leaders. Perhaps that was indeed the case. It is not so now. Political thinking seems since then to have lost any real measure of theoretical or philosophical dimension in England. The educated young seem more absorbed by material rewards and career prospects than they are by discussing critiques of Marxism. Unlike 1977, the allure of the world among the church leadership is now welfare provision and all the other requisites of the moralism of the day. Secularisation is no longer a *political* Trojan horse – it is now the association of human material need with higher idealism. How easily this is made to look like applied Christianity, and how readily the Christian leadership rushes into its arms! The same theological incoherence which characterises the national Protestantism, and renders it incapable of defining religious error, leaves it wide open to the entry of all manner of alien ideology. Secularisation now is the recognition as quintessentially Christian of the priority of welfare materialism – for all its good intentions and common humanity – which now describes such theoretical thinking about the conduct of public affairs as exists.

In the preparatory stages of the English General Election of 2001 there was an emotive and simultaneously ill-informed public debate about the nature of 'the plural society'. Yet a considered understanding of pluralism is essential if the decline of the Church is to be set in any kind of accurate context. Pluralism began when the ancient confessional office of the state first unravelled in the nineteenth century, in a series of *ad hoc* reforms, promoted by Christians who dissented from the State Church, and intended to secure a practical religious equality. Few sought a secular state: they wanted Christian government but without a formal constitutional recognition of one denomination over another. As it happened, the pragmatism of English constitutional practice allowed the Church of England, its back already broken upon the rocks, to survive as a National Establishment – as it does to this day.

Yet it plainly survived as a constitutional *anomaly*. The nineteenth century was also a time when the professional classes and the governing élites persisted in employing institutional Christianity as the vehicle of their moral seriousness. The implications of the constitutional adjustments fed through to the twentieth century however, when the logic of the practical separation of Church and State began to receive more extended political expression. The decline in church attendance, actually dating from at least the middle years of Victoria's reign, also became noticeable in the twentieth century. Numerical decline was uneven: there were occasional minor resurgences of support for Christianity, largely within bourgeois society, as in the 1950s, but they were not sustained. The sudden steep decline of the 1990s seems set to continue; but there will doubtless be a few more hiccups in the process, each one of which, in turn, will be recognised by excited clergy as indications that the 'tide has turned'. There are also some formally successful individual churches. These, however, are distinctly predatory in relation to the church congregations around them, which are, in the process, drained of the meagre support they possess. Successful parishes are largely the beneficiaries of human contrivance – social contacts, 'networking' by the incumbent, 'civic' religion, and other evidences of vitality in a class society. The important feature, the true pointer to what is to come, however, appeared with the conscious acceptance of 'the plural society'. This sprang to life as a distinct and respectable, even fashionable, concept in the 1960s crisis of values.

Pluralism had almost nothing to do with race, or with the existence as English citizens of people of non-Christian religion or culture: the acceptance of the phenomenon preceded the mass immigration of the mid-century, having its roots in the defection from articulate Christianity of large sections of the intelligentsia. A society of plural values is one in which the population – or, in the case of England, the élites whose ideas determine the nature of political and moral discourse – is divided within itself about the moral foundations. Such a society existed quite independently of the race question. In fact the differences of view within the intelligentsia, the governing classes, and their clients and admirers, are less marked than everyone supposes. It is clear, however, that few are any longer prepared, in public life – or, astonishingly, in the Church itself – to contemplate Christianity as the basis of national society. Despite the existence of a State Church, Christianity is no longer perceived to consecrate the operations which lie at the centre of the life of the state. But if the state no longer in practice endorses the Christian religion as the basis of its existence, what higher purpose does it have? Is its concern with the moral and spiritual nurture of the citizens entirely surrendered, and if not, then who can name the ideology or moral system whose application defines the moral authority of the state?

England's celebrated political pragmatism has reached its furthest expression: no one cares to attempt an answer, and the politicians and the educators – and even the clergy – presume that the morality of material welfare is self-evident. The age of ideology, with the *Götterdämmerung* of Marxism and almost every other form of distinct and coherent political thought, is also seemingly at an end – for the time being.

Into this extraordinary void comes an inarticulate and unrecognised materialism, characterised, as authentic materialism always is, by the priority of base human need over the recognition of higher purposes in human association. This position is, of course, suggestively crammed with ideological implications. But none of them are seen. It is in this light that the endorsement by the Church of England of the concept of a society of plural values is to be assessed. It is plainly deeply secularising. As a footnote, let it be added that what is called 'political correctness', to which the Church leaders also pay their full allegiance, is actually an unsystematic application of welfare materialism. Doubtless there is virtue in many of its tenets. It is also not as politically neutral as it is made to appear, and is, in fact, the substitute moral basis brought on to replace the decayed débris of the former Christian state.

A polity which defines its existence around an acceptance of the legitimacy of moral and value diversity, however, is necessarily secular. If the components of the pluralism are to be accorded practical equality and esteem then the state should regard itself as inhibited from endorsing any particular one of them. The government in a society of 'plural values' ought therefore to become less involved with higher moral prescriptions – which will inevitably imply public choice of controverted philosophical propositions – and certainly should regard itself as prohibited from confessing religious truth. To be logical, a society of plural values must have a state structure whose capacity is restricted to questions of safety and public defence, material welfare and utilitarian education, and regulation of such procedures of economic exchange as may address decisions about social equity. In reality, of course, the modern state engages in a seemingly inexorable expansion of collectivist interferences in even the most intimate of social relationships, and often does so for reasons which proclaim their moral virtue – and all at the insistence of a public opinion now educated into expecting a high level of state regulation. What it lacks is any coherence about the pedigree or philosophical authority of the morality whose application lurches forward into increasing expressions of what used to be called totalitarianism. For the government in a society of plural values actually breaks its own canons at the very start: it is a nexus of endorsements of moral orthodoxies – seen most clearly in such matters as race relations, sexual equality, medical ethics or welfare provision. The moral good in these areas does not appear to require explanation; public opinion perceives it to be self-evident. Ideology without a name can be a very acceptable inducement to the surrender of individual liberty.

The leaders of English Christianity appear completely integrated with the common assumptions which sustain acceptance of the 'plural society', largely, it is to be supposed, because they make the common error of defining it almost solely around issues of ethnic, rather than moral, diversity. After nearly two thousand years in which the Church has regarded a unitary state as the normal condition in which to disseminate and transmit truth, it has come now to embrace concepts of pluralism with remarkable enthusiasm. Some of the reasons for this are plainly persuasive enough, but very many are simply confused. In order to appreciate and evaluate the context in which the present internal secularisation of the Church is proceeding, its acceptance of public moral diversity, as being in itself desirable ('enriching society', and so forth), should never stray far from the centre of analysis. The political orthodoxies of the day, in a breathtaking paradox, are acclaimed not as endorsements of selections of social doctrine, nor applications of moral ideas which are so imprecisely defined that they lack a label by which their materialist presuppositions may be identified, but recognitions of simple legitimate diversity. These are difficult times to understand.

EDWARD NORMAN
York, 2001

1

Humanism

Christianity and modern materialist Humanism ought to be at war with each other, and they are not. Why should this be so? The message proclaimed by Christ was about the corruption and sinfulness of men and women, their inability to procure their own redemption, and the forgiveness which he held out to those who repented. It was about an intrinsic bias to evil in human nature which could not be eradicated but whose lamentable consequences could be forgiven. Humanism, in contrast, declares an optimistic view of the capabilities of men and women: they are entitled to moral autonomy, achieve a progressive improvement in the conditions of life on earth, are broadly able to control the human aspects of their development, and are known to possess rights which dignify the individual without the need for reference to any transcendent authority. These two attitudes to human nature are quite simply incompatible. Either humans are internally corrupted and in need of the forgiveness of a divine person, or they are morally autonomous creatures with the capacity for a measure of self-correction.

There are, indeed, Christian thinkers of the modern era who have embraced fundamental aspects of materialist Humanism and identified them as essential applied Christianity. They have tended, sometimes unconsciously, to regard the ideological incompatibilities as merely superstructural, the conditioning of outmoded cultural *dictat,* and have pointed instead to a common agenda of human material need. The Christian love of neighbour, it is argued, is such a supreme expression of the love of God that even those who practise it while rejecting the transcendent tenets of the religion of Christ are in effect doing his work in a manner which is self-evidently authentic. This is to depict Jesus as primarily an ethicist, and in some versions to regard the baneful evidences of human sin, and its universality, as the fruits produced by the rank growths nourished by wrong social systems.

Humanists, for their part, have traditionally shown themselves less accommodating towards religion, which they have assailed as an impediment to human self-fulfilment. In recent times, however, and aware of the decay of support for the teachings of Christianity as conventionally understood, they have espoused a more relaxed attitude to the effects of religion – and have become, in the process, an even greater threat to genuinely spiritual priorities by seeming to remove the ideological precision of a declared foe. The concept of 'spirituality' itself is a telling indicator of what has happened. Once, the word was used solely in relation to the human capacity to enjoy a communion with the divine. Now it is employed to describe merely human aesthetic or emotional experience, the celebration of human artistic or literary accomplishment, an exposition of the finer qualities of individual perception of creativity. The retention of the word 'spirituality' in a secular understanding is thus itself very suggestive.

The notion of humanity as separate from those traditional religious or ideological structures which have accorded life dignity and purpose is too bleak for human vanity, however, and a substitute was inevitable. The practical deification of human accomplishments serves the purpose well. The horrific effects of human wickedness can be attributed by Humanists in large measure to the selfishness of particular social classes or economic systems, thereby rendering the concept of inherent depravity obsolete; and the sacralising of welfare provision and the cultivation of what are now called 'caring' attitudes assume quasi-sacramental status in the new Religion of Humanity. It is scarcely surprising that those Christian thinkers of the present time who have difficulty in subscribing to the miraculous elements of their own faith – like the corporeal resurrection of Christ – can find in the contemporaneous secular enthusiasm for humanity a moralism with sympathetic resonances which does not require acceptance of supernatural belief. Even those with a recognisably orthodox understanding of Christianity are given to acclaiming the essentials of modern Humanism as inherently compatible with religion. For them, attention to suffering achieves ascendancy over any potential risks to spiritual priorities in the elevation of human material needs.

There is also an emphatic tendency within the modern intelligentsia to define ethics in terms of the alleviation of human material suffering: whatever, in medical science, for example, tends to reduce the areas of human misery becomes 'ethical'. Thus a secularised version of the love of neighbour is released from the constraints of an articulated moral system – least of all from one claimed to be of divine origin – and elevates human need as a sovereign principle. Once Christ has been represented as primarily concerned with justice and welfare, rather than with sin and corruption, the equation of his religion with the leading tenets of modern Humanism is easily effected. Humanism, however, in whatever guise it presents itself, is about the sovereignty of humanity and its imagined needs, and not about the demands of God at all. It is not only inherently an enemy of authentic Christianity, but also its probable successor.

The acceptability of Humanist views of human nature is actually facilitated by the non-ideological form in which it is received in modern Western culture. When Marxism was the current vehicle of materialist understandings of humanity it could be readily recognised and fairly easily met in argument – as, for example, in a distinguished sequence of pronouncements made by Pope Pius XII. Philosophical materialism today, however, is not really present to educated opinion as a system of ideas but as an orientation of life and ethical disposition. Once humanity and its needs have been elevated to sovereign determination of public and private action, anything that can be represented as an affront or an impediment to the painless existence of men and women is made to seem morally unacceptable – an outrage. Morality then appears self-evident: it is the palliation of whatever humans themselves regard as the cause of their suffering or deprivation. A set of materialist assumptions about human nature, which comes without an ideology which can be identified and criticised for its actual moral crudity, is plainly persuasive. Among those persuaded, as it seems, are many leaders of Christian opinion. This is additionally puzzling since for centuries the Christian Church, which was founded in an act of expiatory pain, has regarded human suffering as not only inseparable from the nature of life on earth, as a matter of observable fact, but also as a necessary condition in spiritual formation. Since its understanding of the intrinsic depravity of men and women is also central to its salvific mission, the Church should be at the very least unenthusiastic about acclaiming the Humanist agenda as an application of the love commended by Christ. The redemption of souls is a very much more pressing duty than the mere alleviation of the adverse conditions in their lives of which men and women have come to complain. The matter is not quite as stark a contrast as this suggests, however.

The content of the spiritual life is defined for Christians by fulfilling obligations of love towards their neighbour – but those obligations do not arise from a doctrine of human rights: they derive from the command of Christ. The difference is crucial: when Christians come to regard the service of their brothers and sisters as a response to their demands and rights as humans (commonly part of the vocabulary of secular social service) they are easily drawn into the vortex of materialist interpretations of life itself and become inseparable from the prevalent moral culture of the Humanists. Alien views of humanity which come in an obvious form are easily identified and assailed; when they come without an ideological label they are really hazardous. If the common agenda of attending to suffering was the only consideration in the modern equation of Christian service with Humanist ethicism, the potential damage to spiritual integrity might perhaps be slight. But it is not. For the Humanist agenda projects human claims to release from the effects of their own humanity in opposition to the providential scheme ordered by God. The reality is human pursuit of security, and an escalating set of entitlements quite at variance with the Christian insistence that life was not ordained for pleasure or repose.

The crudity of modern Humanism could do with more exposure. Its central contention is that men and women are justified in their self-declared entitlements. There, however, the matter ends. There is no agreement as to what society exists to promote; what individual lives are for. This is especially true in a situation like the prevailing one, in which cultural relativism in a 'plural' society will not allow one view of human destiny, or one religious understanding, to be regarded as more acceptable than any other – at least as far as recognition by the state is concerned. Hence the need, in the gathering Humanist society, for each person to cultivate art and music and such other accomplishments as may indicate that their 'spiritual' persons are still important. Human life becomes an affair of human association itself, and its accessories in family experience and sexual congress; of the pursuit and indulgence of pleasure for its own sake;

of work, in order to meet the costs of family and pleasure; of cultural or recreational diversions to indicate intelligent use of time; of waiting, in lengthening spasms of decrepitude induced by improvements in medical science, for the end to come. In Christian understanding, life is, in all its dimensions, a preparation for eternity, an anticipation of blessedness – because it is an education of the soul – and the conversion of suffering into authentic spirituality. Then the service of others becomes truly the service of Christ himself: and that indeed involves the alleviation of suffering, attention to the disadvantaged, and the advancement of science in order that men and women may join with God in the development of the earth. These ends, in truth, are not sought because of any legitimate human entitlements, nor do they establish men and women themselves as the arbiters of their own sense of worth. Before material welfare comes submission to God, and before submission comes confession of sin, and before that comes an acknowledgement of human worthlessness in the face of the Creator of all things.

Modern people do not feel worthless, however. In addition to enveloping themselves with claims to material well-being and to release from suffering they are full of self-esteem. Here, as it happens, is the probable root cause of much scepticism about the truth of religion found in modern Western society. People experience difficulty in believing the reality of a God who plainly thinks much less of them than they think of themselves. Their estimate of the value of human life is now so great that they are affronted by the existence of afflictions which humanity has always lived with – and has traditionally employed to help give content to spiritual understanding. Modern people, however, conventionally refer to human life as 'sacred'. Yet it is God who is sacred, and life can only be regarded as sacred to the extent that it is a gift from him. There is nothing sacred about individual men and women, even though God calls them to participate in the divine scheme. God alone is a sacred person: people are flawed – intrinsically and in their actions. There is no clearer indication of the arrogance of modern Humanism, of the rebellion against God, of the robbery of divinity, than the supposition that mere people are possessed of 'sacred' qualities. It is, also, difficult to explain evidentially. Humans behave so atrociously, and appear capable of seemingly any measure of evil – and in recent times no less than in the primitive past – that it is hard to see why they judge themselves entitled, as of right, to so many benefits. But they have placed themselves as the sovereign arbiters of their own existence, and modern culture is obsessed by the moral autonomy of the human person and the claims made by people to welfare and repose. In the place of God they worship the human body itself.

At the Dome constructed in London to mark the Millennium, and which was intended to celebrate aspects of national life, it was the 'Body Zone' which attracted by far the largest numbers of visitors. In television programming, similarly, it is dramas about hospitals and the emergency services – minor celebrations, in their way, of the priority of the prevalent culture of safety and health – which attract the greatest audiences. It is trite to say that hospitals have become the cathedrals of materialist Humanism; they are, nonetheless, at the very centre of public consciousness of such moral sense as now attaches to the popular demand for welfare. In one sense this emphasis on the body is simply an interesting resurgence of classic paganism; in another, however, it shows how emphatically people today have come to regard themselves and their welfare as the centre of their perceived moral universe. News items, and features in the media, routinely accord priority to items of health-care policy, critiques of the state of hospital waiting-lists, apparent scandals relating to medical practices, and so forth. People's involvement with the material welfare of themselves, an unavoidable consequence of a materialist culture, is one of the features of the modern

Western world which most clearly points to the elevation of humanity in its own estimation. How can they believe in the existence of God, if God allows life to be arranged in such a fashion that their right to a painless existence is everlastingly frustrated?

From this position there is a ready cross-reference to episodes in the history of Christianity, once represented in heroic terms, which can be judged (in the light of the high estimate now set on the value of the human person) to be inherently discreditable. Thus the Church's support for past social hierarchy, for the Crusades (now considered culturally insensitive, as involving military atrocities, and as flying in the face of modern respect for religious relativity), for the existence of slavery (this despite the plain historical fact that African slavery, for example, was universally practised in black Africa before it was organised by Islamic entrepreneurs), Christian responsibility for various wars, for the subordination of women, for the existence of abuses in charitable institutions conducted by religious authorities, for the Holocaust, and numerous other features of the human record which are now deemed ethically defective. The discrediting of the moral authority of the Christian past has now so completely replaced the representation of the history of the Church as heroic episodes of righteousness and enlightenment – in the schools of the land, and in television documentaries and dramas – that it is hardly to be wondered that attitudes to Christianity are losing the almost automatic respect once very general in public opinion.

What is surprising, however, is the extent to which the leaders of the Church themselves seem prepared to accept this historical revisionism, often made for very questionable reasons and founded on insecure evidence, with little attempt to defend the institution they serve. Their guilty moralism, and their preparedness to apologise for supposed social crimes committed by their distant predecessors, is in extraordinary contrast to the assertive view of their past currently broadcast by leaders of, for example, Islam and Judaism. Their conduct, indeed, amounts to a major secularisation, since the grounds for their new opinions are not derived from Christian re-evaluations of the record but from the general attitudes of a culture which has become soaked in secular moralism.

It is also that common fallacy of the modern moralists: a belief that the protagonists of a past conflict, of ideas or of people, may reasonably be evaluated by reference to current moral norms. This may in fact be done, without having to confess to the adoption of moral relativity, but the operation is much more delicate, and the judgements considerably more refined, than those usually employed today. The destruction of the moral authority of the Christian past not only indicates a Christian loss of confidence in themselves, as an organic body linked directly to the past, but also prepares the way for further dismantling of the authority of the Bible. Passages of Scripture selected for public reading in church these days routinely omit sections believed to offend modern ideals of sex equality, of respect for ethnic diversity, and of acceptable levels of violence. The Church of England has since 1980 set certain passages of the Psalms into square brackets, as candidates for voluntary omission, for precisely these sorts of reason – even though these verses were recited by Jesus himself. The suggestion can only be that modern moral sense is superior to his.

2

Knowledge

It is truly astonishing to realise how quickly the memory of Christian knowledge can be lost. The widespread ignorance of the teachings of the faith now encountered among the young is not a new phenomenon, however. The early philanthropists of the eighteenth century, and the social reformers of the nineteenth, were acutely impressed with the ignorance about Christianity which they discovered among the poor. But they were moved, in consequence, to action. The result was the massive programme of church and school building, and the evolution of an educational mission, which made society at large, by the 1930s, probably the most effectively acquainted with a knowledge of Christian teachings since the early Middle Ages. It was a pretty elementary knowledge, and, as it proved, rather fragile: but a problem in Christian transmission had been recognised and addressed. The visionaries and reformers who established the Church Schools, and whose parliamentary representatives saw to it that the first state schools made provision for Christian doctrines to be taught, also knew something which educationalists of our own day either do not appreciate or do not regard as important. This is that the knowledge of religious teachings, in societies of rapid social and cultural change, is easily lost – and that this loss does not take place slowly, but in a single generation or two. Comparisons may be made with the disappearance of many of the cults of the ancient world: in one lifetime adhesion to the observances and beliefs of a religious tradition could be given up, the children of the former observants being left uninstructed in the doctrines and mysteries of the cult, and their children knowing nothing of them at all.

Modern Britain lives on borrowed time when it comes to a knowledge of Christianity, and the indicators would seem to suggest that that additional time is now running out fast. The schools founded to teach Christianity to children are now often failing to do so, except in the most generalised sense; the institutions of higher education have secularised themselves; the institutional Church has extremely limited access to national or social development – and therefore to a means of influencing educational vision, even if it had the taste for doing so. The teaching profession itself has a liberal disinclination to get involved with the transmission of religious ideas. Such acquaintance with the Christian religion as does inform modern children is largely bereft of doctrinal content and represents the faith in a simple, ethicised form, largely indistinguishable from a check-list of common decencies, or as an explanation of features of heritage passed down from a dead culture. Many parents today are unaware of the extent to which 'religious education' in the nation's schools fails to impart even some of the most basic information about Christian teachings. Indeed, children are more likely to receive a better acquaintance with the ideas of other world religions than they are of the one to which most of them, if only nominally, belong. Because of sensitivity over ethnic issues, furthermore, and a very proper desire to give no offence to the non-white adherents of, for example, Hinduism or Islam, these other world religions, taught as a required part of the curriculum, are presented to the children in a wholly uncritical manner, whereas Christianity is often hedged about with all kinds of reservations touching its supposedly tainted record in social issues and similar matters. It is difficult to determine the effect on the recipients: most are probably confused. But one clear message does come across – that all the world religions are of equal value, and can legitimately claim parity of esteem: in contrast to the exclusivity required by Christianity.

In fact, as it happens, there is a disturbing paradox in the presentation of the other world religions. Whereas Christianity is criticised for its social record in such matters as race equality, sex equality and slavery, the social practices of the other religions – which were anyway reformed through contact with European ideas in the nineteenth century – go largely unexamined. It is not thought helpful to explore Islamic practices in relation to the place of women in society, for example, or to contemplate surviving features of caste hierarchy in Hinduism. What actually happens is likely to be a relativising of all religious teaching, and in endorsing the present arrangements Christian educationalists are unwittingly assisting a defective understanding of their own religion. The law in England requires Christianity to be accorded a special place in the state schools; but this provision is for cultural reasons, as a way of helping children to understand their own national heritage, and not because of any official desire to assist the propagation of Christian doctrines. Doctrines, in fact, are not very consistently brought into the presentation of Christianity in many schools: emphasis is on Christian cultic practices, church buildings and ethical ideas. The law in England also provides for a daily act of worship in the state schools. In very many secondary schools this simply does not happen, and in those where it does it is likely to be an inter-faith meditation of some sort, or a wholly secular ethical disquisition on some matter which has attracted the moralism of the public opinion of the moment.

There should be no doubt about the serious implications for Christianity of the failure to instruct the young in a knowledge of its teachings. Without them, there is no future for the Church.

This disinclination to teach Christianity as confessionally true is understandable as educational policy in a nation which identifies itself as in a condition of moral and religious pluralism. It may seem illiberal to use the authority of the state to further the beliefs of one among a number of competing religious bodies, even in a nation which has a National Church. But what needs to be explained is how the leaders of the Church apply the same judgements of educational intention in the schools conducted under their own auspices, and which were founded explicitly to teach Christianity. For, despite some notable exceptions, the schools run by the Church, both secondary and primary, follow precisely the same practices in relation to the presentation of religion as do the state schools. In them, also, it is considered professionally improper to allow the religious belief of applicants for teaching posts to be a decisive consideration. There, too, Christian doctrines are not presented to the children as truths – there is religious 'education' and not, as formerly, religious 'instruction'. The tenets and practices of religion – of all religions – are explained, and the children are supposed to make up their own minds. Yet the same relativism is not permitted over ethical teachings. The children are not left without guidance on 'correct' attitudes when it comes to issues of race or gender or social distribution. In the Church Schools, as in the state schools, then, Christian *doctrines* remain largely unexplained. How did this situation come about?

It goes back to the report of 1970, produced under the chairmanship of the Bishop of Durham, entitled *The Fourth R*. This document was simply a statement of the then current progressive educational ideas, and in particular an endorsement, for use within Church Schools themselves, of the idea that knowledge of religion should be introduced to the children in a neutral fashion – who could in due time decide whether or not to judge it true. The crucial switch was from confessional instruction to liberal education. It sounded convincing at the time, and promoted, indeed, authentically important features of liberal choice. Educated opinion of the time used the word 'indoctrination' pejoratively; indoctrination, however, is what every ideology needs to practise in order to secure its survival. The concept of liberal choice, admirable in itself, is applicable to mature minds, and not to children. The leaders of the Church accepted the ideas of *The Fourth R,* and they have been virtually unquestioned ever since – a curious example of how uncritical educational theoreticians can be about their own sacral beliefs. The result for the propagation of Christianity has been catastrophic.

There is one simple test. Of all the millions of children educated in Church Schools, how many have adopted Christianity in sufficiently a convinced form as to attend at a place of worship in subsequent life? The thirty years since the ideas of the report were implemented have seen an increasingly steep decline; the existence of the Church in school education has produced ever more negative results, judged, at any rate, by the test of recruitment to church membership. The exponents of the prevailing orthodoxies will of course contend that recruitment was not what they were about. Their ideal was the presentation of educational choice. Children in schools do not think independently for themselves, however, and, as already remarked, they are not allowed to do so over ethical issues. Those who really believe in the truth of their religion will seek, above all things, to transmit it to their young, and this will take an institutional form. Hence the original provision of Christian schools. Yet even schools in the private sector, with a more obvious intention to provide for the propagation of Christianity, have often succumbed to the educational orthodoxies of the times. It should also be noticed that the training of teachers in the Voluntary Colleges of the

Church of England is now in departments of 'Religious Studies' which are themselves, in practical effect, secularised. Staff are often appointed to them on grounds of professional excellence as teachers, and without consideration of their religious beliefs; no attempt is made in them to encourage students to adopt a distinctly Christian approach in the manner in which they will present religion in their subsequent vocations.

Now some will say that it is the duty of Christian parents, in Christian homes, to transmit a knowledge of the faith. And indeed it is; but quite apart from the fact that Christians act collectively, and have accordingly provided educational institutions to assist them in the task, it is increasingly unrealistic to expect that home conditioning will win against the (relativising) effects of the teaching in the schools. Families are actually very efficient at the transmission of values: witness the experience of the former Soviet Union, where after seventy years during which the whole machinery of the state had been employed to discourage religious belief and practice, a remarkably vibrant Christianity emerged fairly intact after its demise. Yet there may be special reasons which explain at least aspects of this social phenomenon, reasons rooted both in the nature of Russian Orthodoxy, and of family life, in a society still considerably unaffected by the diversions of the leisure activities and the material culture which had come to characterise Western societies. Soviet social custom was probably very much less secularised than Western social custom during those years. In the West, as in Britain today, religious belief has been privatised – as it was often by force of political circumstance in the Soviet Union – and also individualised. It is the second of these features which now makes the family a problematical agent for the conveyance of religious belief.

Except when very young, children no longer expect to conform to family values in matters of personal moral or spiritual choice – the dissolvent liberalism of the schools has seen to that. There is also an odd English reticence which often in practice inhibits parents from discussing religion with their children, not unlike their hesitancy and inefficiency in transmitting sexual knowledge. Sunday Schools are in general decline, so either parents undertake systematic doctrinal instruction, or no one does. In effect, no one does. Many believing Christians in the United Kingdom are remarkable for their own lack of precise knowledge about the religious doctrines to which they formally assent; their children are showing that their grasp of them is even less substantial. So although it may be argued that Christian families have only themselves to blame if their children are ignorant of Christianity, it still leaves the phenomenon itself – mass ignorance of religion – as a reality. It may be added, as a footnote, that even those parents who opt to send their offspring to Church Schools do not ordinarily do so for religious reasons. They are worried that the children will grow up without a sound *moral* grounding in decent behaviour: their understanding of Christianity is ethicist and therefore already probably secularised.

3

Ignorance

The ignorance shown by Christians of their own religion is not confined to those with only nominal attachment to the Church. It is widespread, even characteristic, among regular attenders at services. Since these are people who have been exposed to the exhortations and explanations of numerous preachers, it must also say something about the ineffectiveness of a lot of sermons. What it primarily indicates, however, is the extent to which modern people do not expect religion to constitute a structure of doctrine, but to furnish a kind of personal screen on which they can project sympathetic images devised by themselves. In some measure this is itself a reflection of the modern dogma of choice, the questioning of authority (especially authority in ideas), the optimistic self-evaluation which prompts even the most obviously ill-equipped to imagine that they are 'thinking for themselves'. At any rate, they reject the notion of religion as an objectively true set of beliefs and practices, and instead select their own collection of beliefs, and designate the result 'Christianity'. Were it not for the persuasive force of the intellectual fashions inspired by television programmes these would show considerable diversity. In fact there are many common patterns in the way people arrange their own favoured religious and moral ideas, and this can foster the illusion that behind their eclecticism there is folk memory of a once-held uniformity of belief. There survive, still, layers of folk religion, but religious eclecticism is not really an example of them; it is produced by the education of opinion, and is what happens when ecclesiastical authority is so weak, or so disinclined to direct the beliefs of its own adherents, that a luxuriant growth of ideas occurs outside any generally accepted scheme of organisation.

Put quite simply, people who identify themselves as believers have actually devised a menu of ideas and claim the result as Christianity. Thus some are able to believe in the immortality of animals (though by this they generally really mean only their pets), in visitations from the dead, reincarnation, astrology, and a whole catalogue of explanations of mysterious phenomena which they think compatible with Christianity. More damaging, from the point of view of the survival of orthodox doctrinal faith, are the *variants* of authentic belief which they put together: there are those who, with the enthusiastic approval of progressive theologians, engage in undisciplined reductionism. For them, Christian belief does not necessarily involve some of the most fundamental dogmas of the Church, including the resurrection of Christ, the miraculous events of his earthly ministry, and even his divinity.

The Church has always used the intellectual insights and methods of each age, and of each culture through which it has journeyed, to reinterpret its eternal truths. She has often been herself, in the great universities created under her patronage, the source of intellectual enlightenment. But the employment of secular modes of intellectual enquiry whose essential references are intrinsically hostile to religious phenomena cannot be used to reinterpret Christian teachings except in extremely disciplined conditions. And these are in general not available to the men and women in the pews, whose random attraction to diverting ideas picked up from television perusal can be incredibly destructive of traditional religious truth.

It may equally be asked if the learned theologians who undertake very comparable operations in a more informed fashion are actually performing a faithful service to Christianity. At the time of the publication in 1963 of *Honest to God* – a short work by an Anglican bishop, which questioned traditionally-received images of God – it was argued in its defence that more people would retain their Christian faith by a reasonable 'modern' representation of it, than would be offended and quit the Church. But in the years since its publication, and the subsequent publication of numerous comparable works, the volume of church attendance has continued to decline, and in the last decade of the century began to achieve an acceleration which was truly alarming. What is equally alarming is that the sort of radicalism represented by *Honest to God* has now become so commonplace, especially among those who train the clergy, that it passes without remark. In 1963 there was at least a national uproar.

Eclecticism is not the only feature of modern religiosity which is at variance with received Christianity. Church members increasingly expect religion to be emotionally satisfying. There is, of course, a long pedigree to this, and there was even an elegiac quality in the mystery cults of the ancient world. It is absent, however, in the teachings of Jesus, which are not primarily – indeed are hardly at all – addressed to the aesthetic sense of his followers. He did not ruminate on the beauty of the Galilean scenery, nor did he exhort those who would celebrate his truths to compose great art or music. Throughout the Christian centuries church authorities and patrons endowed church buildings with the finest offerings that the art and aesthetic sense of their day could show. They were there, however, not to satisfy the emotional promptings of believers (which was an accidental by-product) but to do honour to God. To some extent, also, the iconography employed had a teaching function in a largely pre-literate age. There were always, of course, ways in which satisfaction of the senses came into this: the point is that the centre of religious allegiance itself was not conceived to involve the satisfaction of mere human sentiment.

People, in general, looked to religion as a means of social identity, as an explanation of their place in the scheme of existence, as a means of avoiding the terrifying prospect of eternal damnation, as the only hope of salvation. None of these, it may be noted, enter very significantly into the reasons a modern person might give for going to church. Romantic taste and sentiment in the later years of the eighteenth century had its spiritual counterpart in the Evangelical movement. Christian adhesion then came to be seen by many as fundamentally an attachment of the emotions – the conversion experience – and as a direct means for the individual to receive consolation from God. Nineteenth-century revivalism, which affected all the churches, popularised the concept; and in the twentieth century, when the emotions became detached from serious purpose, and were often indulged for entertainment, most people ceased to associate them with religion at all. Then, paradoxically, it was this very same secularised understanding of emotional need which those people who for whatever reason had become, or had remained, worshippers in church, began to expect to be 'fulfilled' by Christianity. This is rather an over-simple summary. The point is that evaluating religion as a satisfaction of emotional need, and regarding science and reason, in contrast, as a way of explaining the 'real' world, have since become the conventional categories of explanation which the modern intelligence recognises.

From this conclusion, it was a short step to re-classifying religion as a species of personal therapy: that is the way it is now frequently regarded, in varying degrees of self-consciousness, by many Christian adherents. In such a view of things, there is no need for Christianity to teach fixed or permanent dogmas – anyone can believe anything, provided the central myths can be celebrated in a manner which elevates the individual's sense of 'spiritual' beauty. Here, once again, is the secularisation of the concept of 'spirituality', found as actively in operation among Christian believers as it is a hallmark of modern materialist Humanism.

4

Emotion

With the establishment of the Soviet Union, subsequent to
the Revolution of 1917, there was a problem about what to do
with the church buildings. Some survived in use, under strict
state regulation; most were diverted to secular uses. But
those esteemed for their cultural or aesthetic importance
were preserved as museums. Their interior furnishings –
altars, fonts, iconostases, and so forth – were carefully
labelled to explain their original religious significance to
believers. Enthusiasts of architecture, art and folk-ways
among the Marxist élite, that is to say, were anxious to
preserve Russian heritage and to provide places where the
public could be informed about earlier states of social reality.
Christianity, for them, had exercised social control, and was a
symptom of a wrongly ordered society: the Revolution itself
had made Christianity redundant. The art and design the
churches provided, however, were not only in themselves
redolent of authentic artistic merit – they also expressed past
aspects of historical and social development.

Regarding religion as heritage is what happens when the
state begins to act as a secular agency, and it is what is happening in modern Western societies. When, early in the
1990s, the government in England began to make grants of
public money available for the restoration and conservation
of the great religious buildings, it was not because a National
Church existed, and was entitled in any sense to support

from state resources; nor was it in recognition of a higher calling in the life of the state. The grants were made to preserve and to popularise heritage, not religion. Astonishingly, the leaders of the Church have themselves come to accept the same agenda of heritage priorities, and now suppose that it is possible to use their cathedrals and historic parish churches to mediate religious faith through their architectural and artistic features. Up go the labels and signs, at altars and shrines, to explain their cultic significance to visitors; the buildings themselves are believed to declare 'spirituality' through their very stones.

At the simplest level of understanding this acceptance of the objectives of the heritage agenda is, from a Christian perspective, questionable. To the extent to which the great cathedrals and churches are symbols of faith – and not of the territorial ambitions of a former social order, signs of the wealth of entrepreneurs, the results of fashions of taste, or canopies over the remains of the dead – they are *merely* symbols. To work, to be activated, it is necessary for there to be a prior knowledge of the ideas symbolised. And against the grain of much nineteenth-century romanticism, and the twentieth-century *penchant* for art history, it is most likely that cathedrals and churches were not originally intended as free-standing embodiments of faith. They do not, and were not intended, to explain what Christianity is all about. They are, it is true, a mixture of functionalism and iconography – but the purpose was never to provide 'sermons in stone', as Christian explanation in our own day likes to suppose: they project at best only very fragmentary dimensions of the Christian message. To use them as a key to understanding the religion is extremely partial. The fact is that Christianity is a set of doctrines which are sublime and living. The art and design of buildings is static and confined to the ages which produced them. It is quite possible to illustrate the Christian faith by reference to features in great churches, but the result will be very much less satisfactory, and certainly less complete, than simple doctrinal explanation. A society unin-structed in what Christianity is actually all about – the supreme drama of the forgiveness of human sin and the redemption of the race – will only appreciate its symbolism when it has received instruction in the truths symbolised. It would, perhaps, not matter if modern churchpeople were prepared, as they are, to accept the heritage route – of pre-senting the faith in the partial images available in their buildings – were it not for other aspects of heritage conserva-tion which in themselves promote a secular understanding.

First among these is the confusion of aesthetic sensation with authentic spirituality: that is to say, spirituality as a consequence of the proximity of the individual to the divine Being, and not as a pursuit of inward significance. To go into a great church and to be moved in the emotions or the aes-thetic sense by the spaces and decorative devices is actually a worldly phenomenon. The emotions can be moved by seem-ingly anything the individual has been conditioned to value as inspiring. There is also social conditioning. This is a class society, and the leisure pursuits and aesthetic senses of the social classes develop largely in parallel. Thus the bourgeois response to a great church building is likely to be the evoca-tion of beautiful feelings and literate associations; that of a person from less literate sections may well begin with a degree of wonder at the work of men's hands, but will rapidly advance to wonder at scale, craftsmanship, quaint features, tombs, and so forth. Most visitors to cathedrals, for example – as becomes clear from questions addressed to information points – want to know if there are coffins in the crypt, or where the shop is. The class nature of responsiveness to church visits is actually also indicated by the non-religious use made of the buildings. The Deans and Chapters of cathe-drals, and the incumbents of parish churches, are in general quite happy to allow performances of secular music, provided it is identifiably 'serious' in purpose, classical or modern. That is because they associate aesthetic sensation with religious experience: for them, the emotions evoked by Beethoven or Mahler legitimately convey religion. But most would not allow performances of secular pop music. Yet it is difficult to see why. If secular musical concerts are acceptable in sacred buildings, then the judgement that 'serious' pieces are somehow compatible with the religious character in ways that popular music is not requires explanation. There are clear social class resonances here, since cultural accidents have resulted in classical music having a numerically smaller following in working-class society than popular music.

Emphasis on heritage considerations also involves leaders of the Church in an almost unavoidable identification of the Christian message with dead culture. Most cathedrals, for example, have schools visits programmes. These are centres, under the auspices of the church authorities, which arrange for parties of schoolchildren to receive conducted tours of cathedrals and have the various features of the buildings explained to them. The centres are very professionally organised, and it has now become usual for the staff employed in them to be trained primary schoolteachers. Though employed by the cathedral, however, it has also become usual for those conducting the tours to adopt the same detached attitude to religious education as is now regarded as professionally appropriate in a large majority of schools in England: the children are not to be presented with Christianity as true, that is to say, but as one among a number of religious phenomena, or as an important element in the inherited national culture. So although a moment for quiet reflection is included in many of the schools visits programmes in cathedrals, the basic intention is a backgrounding in historical, social and cultural evidences of former states of society. For secondary schools, this is linked to the provisions of the National

Curriculum. In practice, therefore, the church authorities are subsidising a largely secular understanding of their buildings, and simply hoping that any children whose aesthetic sense happens to be activated in some fashion by their visit to the building will associate it with religious belief. This is, in the nature of things, what does sometimes happen – but it is not a conveyance of Christianity.

The acceptance of public money for building works has also placed a question mark over the future of the cathedrals. Legislation already requires the authorisation of Fabric Advisory Committees – of which the Dean and Chapter are not members – before any structural work may be undertaken, and this extends to any interior fixture. English Heritage, which is an agency of the state, is the main disposer of money for restorations. It is plain that they will in future need each cathedral to have a Conservation Plan, covering the entire building and its annexed facilities, and approved by them, before cash will be authorised. The Church, therefore, has in practice lost control of much of the care of cathedrals to a secular body, and it is probably just a matter of time before the state takes over directly. It is only a small number of the ancient foundations which have reasonable wealth; most cathedrals are in a dire financial condition. The future fate of all the cathedrals will probably be decided uniformly, however, and it is difficult to see how the Church can avoid an eventual transfer to English Heritage directly. The introduction of admission charges at some cathedrals may slightly have postponed their loss of independence – but only slightly. The charges have actually made them subject to market forces in the tourism business, and to the numerous and growing regulatory requirements mandatory for those whose premises are open to the public on a commercial basis. The accumulating costs of health and safety, disabled access, fire regulations, and various layers of planning permission, can only be met by the larger and more prestigious cathedrals.

When the buildings are eventually transferred to English Heritage, when the last tune is called, the Church of England, or Christian bodies of any sort, are unlikely to receive special privileges in their future use. In a society of 'plural values' – which church leaders themselves are always anxious to endorse – the buildings will probably be reserved for serious cultural purposes, such as secular concerts and secular weddings, and doubtless also will be booked by various religious bodies for services. This is not the distant future; it is what lies perhaps twenty years ahead.

There are implications here for future parochial strategy. With declining numerical support for many urban parishes has come financial collapse. Some, as a result, are suggesting that large numbers of churches in cities might be closed and the local cathedral turned into a kind of super parish church. Recent cathedral reform has independently stimulated the adoption of parochial-style ministries by Deans and Chapters, so the ground has in one sense already been prepared for such a redeployment of urban church resources. But with the distinct possibility that the Church will lose control of the cathedrals in the years that lie ahead, a strategy which envisages the use of the cathedrals as co-ordinating parochial institutions would plainly be mistaken. The church authorities, on the contrary, might start looking at the church buildings in cathedral cities to determine which of them could become cathedrals in place of the historic buildings which will by then have become museums of heritage and concert halls. The opportunity might be taken to designate churches in centres of population rather than in the ancient sites where the old cathedrals are often situated. In Sussex, for example, a large church in Brighton could replace Chichester as the Anglican cathedral of Sussex. No one, however, appears to be thinking in these radical terms, since no one, in the Church of England, seems to appreciate either the seriousness or the proximity of secularisation.

The main problem about the association of the Christian mission with the popularity of the heritage industry remains simple ideological confusion. And that is why it is such a powerful incentive to the further internal secularisation of the Church. With seemingly irresistible momentum, the clergy and lay ministers, and the Christian schoolteachers and the religious broadcasters, are insistent in believing that Christianity can be conveyed – often almost exclusively – through cultural representations. Behind this lies the supposition, so widespread with the intelligentsia of the times, that science and modern knowledge are all about reality, and that religion is all about the emotions; that objective truth is to be sought entirely in the realm of material explanation, and that religious 'experience' resides in personal sensation and aesthetic appreciation; that real data about the nature of things, so to say, excludes the 'poetic' faculties which are catered for by religious belief. Authentic Christianity, in complete contrast, is centred in doctrinal truths which are known about through the transmission of a living company of adherents, and is in no sense dependent upon the emotional condition of the individual. Christ did not talk about aesthetic experiences but about sin, repentance and redemption. His body in the world, the Church, has for two millennia found that a knowledge of these things needs to be taught *directly* to the people – it is only in our own day that we have come to regard art history or past folk perceptions of faith to be the most appropriate method. As an aid to understanding, the evidences of heritage have some minor advantages; when they come to preoccupy the manner in which the Christian religion is represented to the age, there is a real threat to the integrity of the faith.

Christianity is about the demands of God and the obligations which are owed to him by his creatures: it is not about the emotional satisfaction of men and women. It is characteristic of Humanist materialism, with its emphasis on the sovereign needs of the person, that a receptivity to any recreational activity – which is how people today envisage religious observance – involves pleasant sensations. A religion which is centred in sin and judgement does not appeal; one whose 'beautiful' emotional tableaux flatter individual self-significance does. Modern people have also come to regard the pursuit of pleasure as the main purpose of their lives, and they see no reason to exclude religion, if they bother with religion at all. Their understanding of goodness involves the concept of 'caring' and there is no reason why, in the present cultural climate, they should associate this with religion. Secular agencies of the state have taken over in the realms of welfare provision. So an understanding of religion has become expressed almost entirely in terms of emotional appeal. It is the market rate. Church leaders, for their part, have been only too accommodating, and have rushed to identify the Christian message with personal emotional satisfaction. For the more educated, a kind of higher perception of pleasure resides in great music and heritage and art: this is the form that the Church now adopts to present its message. Instead of adorning the faith, however, their efforts only tend to secularise it.

5

Pluralism

There was a time when the culture of the nation was so informed with Christian knowledge, and so infused with ideals of Christian order, that when the Church recognised its aspirations it listened largely to the return of its own voice. But in modern times the culture has become secularised, and the leaders of the Church, in persisting to follow its ideals, are becoming themselves secularised in the process. In a class society like the present one, furthermore, the dominant enthusiasms of the bourgeois liberals are those which are most likely to be reproduced within the various responses of the Church. For this is the class, together with recruits and clients from other social classes (who have undergone embourgeoisement), whose preoccupations are embodied within the institutions. Sometimes, it is true, the bourgeoisie are divided ideologically among themselves. In most circumstances, however, it is the more progressive thought which attracts the church leaders – terrified of appearing to be old-fashioned, or to be out of touch with what is perceived to be youth culture, or because they simply reflect the values of the social sections from which they are themselves largely drawn. That this places them within an élite of self-conscious social progressivism, and therefore often removed from authentic working-class culture, has never appeared to worry them. Their employment of popular rhetoric seems sufficient in itself to disguise from them the fact that the actual ideas they adopt are characteristic of the prevailing liberalism of the intelligentsia. In the 1960s, leading theologians spoke quite frankly about the Church 'learning from the secular'; it was a period when some advanced to acclaim what they called 'the death of God'. The 1960s also saw the popularity within the church leadership of 'Liberation Theology' – despite its starkly Marxist philosophical pedigree, drawn from its applications in Latin American urban dissidence and in African anti-colonial wars. The Marxist social analysis was, indeed, ideologically sophisticated: this was the part which the Western admirers of Liberation Theology, and their British enthusiasts, tended not to understand. Their acclamation was of the ordinary social progression explicit in the programmes of the Christian revolutionaries; there was a pervasive romanticism in the images of a struggle for freedom that seemed, falsely as it turned out, to place the Church on the side of the people. The people, in due time, turned to conspicuous consumerism rather than to Marxist virtue, and Liberation Theology, despite the nostalgic enthusiasm its memory still evokes in programmes used in Anglican ministerial training, has translated itself to the periphery.

The 1990s equivalent of the 1960s political radicalism was 'political correctness' – sexual equality, disabled rights, inclusive social structures, racial integration, cultural parity and so forth. The ideals of political correctness are ostensibly devoid of political partisanship; in reality, however, they amount to the political application of the pervasive but ill-defined Humanism. The coping stone is the concept of the 'plural society'. It is no surprise to find the leaders of the Church among the most enthusiastic advocates of the concept; once again they are echoing the ideals of the bourgeois intelligentsia. Political correctness is in reality also classic Puritanism: a moralistic creed which all are compelled to adopt through legislative action. Yet the 'plural society' is an extremely confused concept, to which few have attempted to give philosophical or theoretical clarity. The leaders of the Church seem to have identified it with racial equality, to which it does have a limited relationship since some of the cultural differences involved in the notion of social pluralism are of ethnic origin. In essence, however, the 'plural society' is about the acceptance, because it is in itself desirable, of differing life-styles, belief systems, and, so it declares, of different values throughout society. It indicates the abandonment by social and political authority of prescriptive uniformity in a number of areas where once there had been recognised norms: religion, sexual morality, cultural value, gender identification.

The state is envisaged as a mechanism to protect the various sections, and it should not legitimately be employed to give its authority exclusively to any one of them. It is conceived to be the duty of a democratic polity that majority rule must have legally defined limits, so that minority beliefs are protected. There shall be positive legal action, on the other hand, to promote the concept of equality between the diverse components of society – as in the legislative requirement, for example, that building regulations enforce disabled access, or in the use of the school programmes to teach children approved views about race equality.

Why does the Church seek to associate itself so closely with the ideals of the plural society? Through most of its history, in fact, the leaders of Christianity – like the leaders of Judaism and Islam – have taught exactly the reverse. The state was then conceived as an instrument to protect truth, even when the guardians of truth within society were numerically inferior. In civilised society toleration was conceded to dissenters, but only in the degree to which the practice of dissent posed no threat to the survival of the state. In the Byzantine world and in the West this scheme of things became the 'Christendom model': community was recognised as aspiring upwards, and became, in fact, an icon of the celestial society. The sovereign was the earthly representative of God's order. The secularisation and democratisation of the last two centuries has despatched all that – or nearly all of it. In England there is a surviving National Established Church, a provision by the state for the teaching of Christian truth. Though this is arguably highly anomalous, there are many within the leadership of the Church of England who still contend for the utility of an Establishment of religion. Extraordinarily, however, these are also those who are enthusiastic about the ideals of a plural society. Yet the two concepts are plainly incompatible. Establishment is a sign of state preference for one religion over others, and however greatly it is in practice broadened, so that the state comes to recognise a diversity of faiths, *any* connection of the law and religious opinion still constitutes an establishment of religion, and discloses an official recognition of religious belief in society.

Let it be supposed, for purposes of analysis, that the frequent endorsement of the concept of a plural society made by Christian bodies, and by prominent church dignitaries, is to be taken seriously. What are they actually supporting? The state which presides over a plural society is presumably one which interferes as little as possible with the beliefs and practices of the citizens – whose right to diversity is, after all, what the whole thing is about. The ideas of Jews and Christians and atheists and blacks and whites and disabled and underachieved are all equal and to be treated with equal esteem. Different cultures are all the same: aboriginal art is as good as Michelangelo. But in reality, in order to achieve this practical equality, the state has begun to regulate huge areas of social exchange once regarded as exclusively within the determination of individuals. The state, instead of being a neutral arbiter between the competing elements of the social pluralism, is actively engaged in a collectivist explosion of legislative promotion of approved attitudes and practices. In issues such as race relations, employment policy, parenting, disablement, women's rights, medical ethics, and so forth, the state now routinely prescribes and enforces extremely precise 'correct' attitudes, and employs every means of propaganda at its disposal to do so. The state in a plural society, indeed, is turning out to be the old confessional state in a new guise, and with infinitely enhanced powers. It is no longer the Christian religion which the authority of the state protects and promotes, but a species of undefined Humanism. What is clear, indeed, is its *secularity*.

All of the collectivist advances in the regulation of social relationships are made for unstated ethical reasons, but the ethics being enforced are plainly secular ethics. That is the only way they can be acceptable in a society of plural values. Because they are left undefined it is up to each section of the pluralism to identify itself with the various areas of state regulation. The Church is not only active in doing that – acclaiming each episode of state welfare advance as an exemplification of the love of neighbour enjoined by Christ – but it also identifies itself with the entire concept of the plural society at the same time. As it does so it unavoidably secularises its own understanding of social action. It reinvents itself as the advocate of an ethical consciousness which is so generalised that it can be regarded as virtually indistinguishable from the ethical beliefs of other religious bodies, or from the secular ethicism of the intelligentsia. And, again, social class resonances are heard. The issues which excite the moralistic attention of the bourgeois liberals are, as in the past, the areas which in the end leave the basic and determining structures of society intact. There is no association here with the realities of genuine social change, as there is not, either, in modern British Labour politics. The obsessive inclination to inaugurate social righteousness is all about things like women's rights, race equality and the levels of health-care provision. Few now seem to be interested in the social dynamics of radical economic distribution and exchange, the reappraisal of false-consciousness, or the reality of class conflict.

The 'plural society' is indeed not some amazing new piece of modern inventiveness: it is society in transition. It represents the decay of one set of social orthodoxies and their replacement by another. Because the eventual outcome is not yet clear – no more than the appropriateness of the means by which social leaders seek to control the process of its advancement is clear – the shape of the new society remains unspecified. This is in correspondence with the intellectual or theoretical pedigree of the ethics of the plural society. They are clearly Humanist, but very few see this with any coherence of vision, and the compulsive moralism of the advocates of social diversity rests upon a virtually uncontested assertion that intrinsic human goodness is evenly expressed in all the cultures of the general mixture. The unpleasing reality, however, is that some cultural expressions are highly unsuitable as candidates for inclusion. European fascism in the twentieth century, for example, conveyed cultural ideas, and on a scale which indicated mass democratic approval, which have now to be excluded, on moral grounds, from the reality of a plural society. And so the plural society represents a selection. Who determines the selecting process, and for what sorts of theoretical reasons? The question is not addressed. It is simply assumed that a kind of Natural Law operates; they are self-evident.

Thus ethics comes to be defined around hedonism – the good is reduced to whatever is perceived conducive to human happiness. Cultural excellence becomes the best that is promoted by each of the components of the social pluralism, with no obvious pointer to any objective standard or any indebtedness to traditional values. And religion, where it is considered at all in relation to social association or the composition of the state, is reduced to cultic sensation – it is the emotional satisfaction of people who for historical reasons have come to experience 'spirituality' in different ways. Out of this moment of transition, and of its accompanying theoretical incoherence, some new structural expression will doubtless in due time appear. Then we shall hear no more of the 'plural society', and the state will resume its normal function, in human development, of compelling uniform adhesion to its values. This is already beginning to happen, of course, but the theoretical imprecision of the ethical basis of the compulsion, and the chance that the available Humanist ethics do not at the present time have an identifiable philosophical label by which they can be identified, disguises the velocity of the transition.

Into this confusing disintegration of familiar values, with the baying acclamation of the new social and moral virtues obtruding on every side, the leaders of the Church of England have wandered, like hares before lions. Their conversion to the new orthodoxies has been, nevertheless, instantaneous. No one has been louder in their denunciations of the old confessional state, of the structure of traditional Christendom, with its unitary purposes and its clear advocacy of Christian morality. No one, either, has been so insistent in identifying the ideals of cultural diversity as embodiments of human goodness. And no one, in consequence, more earnestly heaps approval on the massive accumulation of state collectivist powers by which the ideals of the neo-Humanism are being enforced – all the laws by which racism and sexism and insensitivity to various social unfortunates are specified as the new sins. Most of the social attitudes which are now being made the subject of regulatory correction are, it need hardly be said, very disagreeable – and some, even, are sins. But who said that the modern supposedly liberal state should be the undeclared instrument of a materialist theocracy? How did it happen that housewives who neglect their children for a couple of hours will see them taken 'into care' by the state, or that individuals who download child pornography from their computers will be sent to gaol? The dogmas of the plural society, as they receive legislative expression, are creating a new moral autocracy – not a new liberalism. It is this neo-Puritanism which the Church is now identifying as applied Christianity, and which amounts, indeed, to the consecration of the secularisation of moral value – a strange paradox. Sometimes, as it happens, leaders of the Church are merely acting opportunistically, associating the faith with transient moments of popular moral outrage generated by a particular crime, or television documentary, or disaster. The Church has long since lost control of the moral climate, and now appears to react to events in the same manner of passion and sensation as the public in general. It has become a reactor to the unfolding of the components of modern moral seriousness, and not a significant contributor. Its genius for locating human misery in the spiritual frailty of individual humans, which once lay at the heart of its social message, has faded with the ghostly images of a former age.

6

Secularity

People in Western societies are now so accustomed to living in a secularised social culture that they find societies governed by religious convention truly shocking. Thus the prevalent attitudes to Islamic fundamentalism: the renewed ordering of the details of daily life according to religious precept seems barbarous to those who exist without any particularly religious frame of reference. Even more difficult for them to understand is that the rejection of Western secular values, and the revival of religious observances, has taken place in cities – and in some of the cities of the Middle East which, due to oil wealth, are among the most advanced in material facilities. Past analysis had seemed to indicate that it was 'backward' rural areas which retained religious folk-ways, and that there was a definite link between urbanisation and secularisation. When, in 2001, the Taliban authorities in Afghanistan carried out a systematic campaign of destroying ancient effigies of the Buddha – regarded as blasphemous denials of Islamic teaching – there was an uproar among Western observers, not because they cared very much about religion but because a kind of secular sin was being perpetrated against artistic objects. It illustrated well the chasm between the modern Western secular mind and the outlook of a movement which regards religious truth as more important then aesthetic taste. To some extent, also, the conflict between the communities in Northern Ireland is incomprehensible in England, because the English secular politicians cannot cope with people who take religion seriously.

The English Church has to operate in a situation of deep, and deepening, secularity. Expressed in its greatest simplicity, this means that daily life is largely bereft of reference to religion. Extraordinarily, individual Christians seem to be little aware of just how secular their own lives have become merely by being integrated with the encompassing social norms. The Church, collectively, appears unwilling to attack the prevalent culture for its lack of religious reference – even when addressing its own members, even when seeking to instruct believers themselves in how to live Christian lives. At the top of society the state itself has a number of symbolical survivals of its Christian past, but politicians extremely rarely propose courses of public policy, or seek to explain their actions, by reference to religion. The dogma of the 'plural society' increasingly makes such reference, anyway, appear inappropriate. Political action is declared very self-consciously for 'moral' reasons, and there is a widespread requirement that 'morality' must inform the conduct of politicians. But the nature of the morality so frequently invoked remains unidentified; few claim it to be distinctively Christian – though there is an acknowledgement that former Christian teaching constitutes part of national heritage.

This attitude pervades the whole of society. Parents at home, and teachers in the schools, give moral exhortation to children which is based, not on Christian belief, but on an appeal to self-interest. Do not do this-and-this, they say to the young (and to one another), because you would not like it done to you. God's law rarely comes into it. There is now no higher note at the centre of the life either of society or the state. In reality, of course, this indicates the practical displacement of Christianity by secular Humanism, but no particular intellectual process has prepared for this outcome, and even in educated opinion there is very little awareness that this is what has happened. Secular morality is, to some extent, Christian precept without acknowledgement, a sort of religionless Christianity of the variety advocated by *avant garde* theologians in the 1960s. But the morality conveyed within the Christian religion is not itself the essence of the faith – which is about the sovereignty of God, the corruption of humanity, and the sacred gift of redemption.

The ethics taught by Christ were not the authentically original part of his message: they provided ways of testing belief and giving content to the life of Christian service. They were not in themselves the supreme purpose of the coming of God into the world, and they were, indeed, a compilation and revision of familiar moral teaching drawn from Jewish tradition – itself influenced by the diverse cultures with which the people of Israel had become acquainted through exile and conquest. Modern secular ethics are not respected by populations today because they bear a resemblance to Christian ethics, however, but because they are thought to express universal patterns of behaviour which unite all people in a common humanity and procure welfare benefits. The means by which this self-interested hedonism is conveyed, in point of moral rhetoric, is called 'caring'. The English Church seems to have identified itself more or less completely with this essentially secular frame of reference. The pronouncements of bishops or of church bodies on moral questions are made with increasingly rare mention of religious authority; they reflect, indeed, the general and secular moral sense. Bishops who opposed the liberalisation of the Sunday trading laws, for example, did not do so because of the injunction about Sabbath observance in the Ten Commandments, but because they were a potential threat to family life, and to the health benefits of a day of rest.

Every now and again political parties re-examine the electoral appeal which they think may reside in claiming a religious identification for their programmes. This does not usually amount to much, and sometimes even derives from the chance that a particular leading politician happens to attend church. The possibility that an individual's or a party's political policies will be formulated by reference to a distinct Christian creed is remote. The conventions attendant upon 'plural society' pieties, and the imprecise manner in which what is thought of as 'Christian' teaching is grasped, together almost guarantee that religion will have no real place in the formation of politics. The plain fact is that there is a consensus that the maintenance of the integrity of the family, or 'family values', is at the centre of political duty. The leaders of the Church are among the most vociferous in declaring the importance of the family as a basic Christian unit – and this despite the absence of clear teaching on the matter in the Gospels. The family, as it happens, does not have any values. The family is merely a social device which is notably effective at transmitting whatever values achieve sacral authority at a particular moment in social evolution. It is a matter of historical record that the family has acted in this way to transmit all kinds of values, some of them, in traditional society, with very baneful consequences. The model projected in descriptions of family values, and of the family as a unit, tends to be that of the bourgeois families of the first half of the twentieth century. A lot of it is plain social myth, anyway. But above all, it is secular. When the family was respected because it was part of God's order it was a unit with a patriarchal head, a marked absence of women's rights, and a disinclination to countenance individual dissent from its loyalty code. What church leaders now endorse as 'Christian' family values are really just the ordinary secular decencies which are supposed to provide the stability now considered essential for the effective rearing of children.

Only in a very small number of homes, even of convincedly Christian homes, does the manner of modern living encourage a specifically religious existence. It depends, of course, on how a 'religious existence' is understood; but where there is a very low level of reference to religious belief in the exchanges and choices which constitute communal association, it can be taken that secular alternatives are in operation. A simple test: how many modern parents give their children any kind of instruction in Christian doctrines? There is no reliable data for an answer, but the supposition, in view of the results (judged by later adhesion to any Christian body), is that very few do. Nor will children receive a knowledge of the Bible, or experience of prayer, at vast numbers of schools in this country, since the legal provision for these things is in so many places unobserved. What the children do get – in school, on the television screen, and by association with the values propagated by advertising – is a set of secular moral norms, often incoherently presented, usually made through appeals to self-interest, which provide a seemingly satisfactory and rather surreal substitute.

When daily life is bereft of references to religion it can scarcely be expected that religion will be regarded as a significant part of the culture. In reality the presentation of religion is increasingly negative. Christianity is now often represented, in television and journalism, and in the classroom, as the author of many wrong attitudes in traditional society. It is regarded, often with very insubstantial historical backing, as tainted with racism, sexism, social conservation, as the agent of slavery, of persecution, and of a large catalogue of evils identified by modern Humanism as inhibiting social progress. The piecemeal destruction of the moral authority of the Christian past is an essential preliminary to the displacement of Christianity by secular Humanism, and it is a process which is well established.

The privatising of religion is also reaching new dimensions. In the 'plural society' the state has necessarily to regard religious belief as a matter of individual preference, and morality couched in religious terms with it. Yet the state requires a moral basis for its own authoritative action: all law, to be obeyed, posits a prior moral purpose, even when it is very indirectly discerned. The modern state is no longer inclined to legislate on the basis of a morality which is distinctively Christian, and it certainly would no longer envisage the use of law to encourage or to enforce Christian religious belief. But it does legislate and enforce secular morality: the supposedly agreed tenets of Humanism are recognised as legitimately enforceable because they are in the best interests of the citizens. Religion, however, is now a private matter, no more a legitimate concern for government promotion than astrology or gardening. Christian believers themselves have become impatient of the concept of religious authority – not just as formerly exercised by the state but as provided within the Church. Fewer and fewer expect to be instructed in doctrines or interpretations. Religion is becoming so individualised that 'believers' expect to be able to make up their own understanding of Christianity, often by random selection from current ideals, some traditionally recognised within the Church and some not. The same is apparent in their attitude to Christian moral teaching: here, too, on issues such as divorce or abortion, modern Christians like to exercise their own judgement. The data on which their selection is made is in general furnished by television presentations of the issues involved or feature journalism. It is rarely supplied by resort to the vast body of Christian moral theology. Once again, the secular enters the choices of Christians, and modern privatised religion inevitably turns out to be an affair of sentiment, emotional satisfaction, aesthetic sensation and welfare. It is not often based upon the doctrines maintained by the Church through the centuries.

Because secularisation in England does not result from the application of an ideology, or derive from an assault upon religion, and is a practical reorientation of life produced gradually, drip by drip, in a piecemeal abandonment of traditional observances, it has not been resisted in any systematic fashion. People rather regret what is happening, but are unprepared to do anything about it – especially as the Churches seem so ineffective. Their lives are passed in a gentle materialism, and the entertainment and even drama which religion provided in traditional societies is adequately catered for in modern substitutes. The provision of entertainment in society today, in fact, is so abundant, and the money to pay for it is so accessible to ordinary people, that if there were no other explanations to hand, this alone would account for the empty churches. It used to be said that at least religion retained a monopoly of the rites of passage. This, too, is changing. The baptism of infants is no longer regarded as a conventional accompaniment of birth; the declining statistics of baptism show no sign of halting. Recent legislation which allowed secular venues to be recognised as places for legal marriage ceremonies has revealed that many of those who had before chosen a church wedding had done so for the picturesque ceremony and its associations rather than out of religious conviction. Secular funerals are increasingly common, especially among the more educated social sections. Even funeral rites performed in churches are now expected to dwell more upon the virtues and humanity of the deceased, and on the emotional state of the survivors, than on the awesome judgement that is to come and the hope of God's mercy. A service which celebrates an individual life, and in consequence personalises a rite whose very essence had, in the old Prayer Book, emphasised that death and judgement are the same for everyone, sets human priorities and therefore necessarily secularises the occasion. The clergy themselves are often the initiators in converting funerals into acts of grief therapy rather than preparations for divine judgement.

Modern people have actually shown that they can get on very well without religion. Many in the Church find this puzzling, for they suppose that there exists a kind of interior disposition in each person to need religious sentiment – the Evangelicals sometimes call it, in their way, a 'God-shaped hole'. But this is a mistaken notion. The human inclination to satisfy an interior sense of emotional need is an acquired characteristic; it is cultural. People are simply taught from birth that they are significant and that they have emotional needs that can be accommodated by some higher reflective capacity. People would appear to have the capability of being programmed for virtually anything – hence the importance, always recognised in Christianity, to nurture children in authentic faith from the beginning of their lives. Children reared in a wholly secular culture will have wholly secular expectations, emotional and actual. Is a *wholly* secular culture possible? Or will there always be persistent survivals of religious conditioning, transmitted through received modes of thought and behaviour? Probably not: the evidence so far seems to indicate that secular sacral values are just as effective as ones represented within a religious tradition in adhering people to approved social purposes. And at the level of emotions, it seems clear that aesthetic sensation, or the manipulative effects of, for example, popular music or drugs, is a perfectly adequate substitute for religion. Authentic religion – the true understanding of Christianity – is not about emotional satisfaction, or what belief can do for the sentiments of the individual: it is a duty owed to God because he exists. It is not about us, but about him. Alas, once more, modern Christians themselves are among the first to get their priorities wrong, and they often set out to propagate the message of Christ in a manner which presents it as the answer to human emotional need. The experience of secular-isation in Western societies is indicating that such a need can be met in other ways; ways, furthermore, which are less demanding and more rapidly achieved.

The multiplicity of secular substitutes for religion, therefore, does not indicate, in the Positivist sense, that humanity has an inbuilt requirement for something like faith. It shows, on the contrary, that faith has often, even by its own adherents, been wrongly understood as supplying needs which derive in fact from particular prior conditioning. The Marxists have always said that religious belief indicates the existence of a wrongly ordered society; once society has been rationally organised, the need for faith will disappear as a social phenomenon. The observation, stripped of its unnecessary annexure to Marxist dogma about proletarian eschatology, is true enough. It is true, that is to say, of the use commonly made of religion by those concerned with social control, and does not affect the question of whether Christianity is true in itself.

Christianity, as it really is, needs for its survival to be taught to each person and to each generation, as true in itself, and as dependent for its authority on uniquely revealed knowledge. It is not effective because it fills an intrinsic need – had it been so it would indeed have been no more than just another candidate for occupancy of the false consciousness of the people. Christianity is in the market-place of competing ideas: its survival is not because of its appeal – or its fulfilment of human need – but because it is rational. It is an account of the Creator and his involvement with the Creation; and about human fallibility and human redemption. The emotional condition of people, and their liability to believe seemingly everything they are conditioned to believe, does not come into it. In the transition from state confessionalism based upon religion to the confession by the state of secular ethics, people will continue to experience a need for what they had been conditioned to expect: occasions when social and moral values are celebrated. So there will be, at least for a time, substitutes for religion, and they are accumulating quickly in modern Western society. They do not, however, indicate any intrinsic human need for substitutes;

they simply fill a gap which has opened up in the transition period. Symbolical observances are powerful social and political cohesives anyway: not in fulfilment of interior compulsions but because the organisers of society recognise their effectiveness, in the positivistic sense, of promoting their ideals.

The many secular substitutes for religion are therefore surface phenomena. But they indicate a real decline in social adhesion to Christianity. They are also truly secular: this is not religion under an alternative set of evidences. Some are familiar: thus the gradual elimination of references to religion in media debates about the 'great moral issues' of the day. Some are structural, like the secularisation of the concept of charity. The annual celebration known as 'Comic Relief', which is heavily promoted by the BBC, is a clear example of exhortation to charitable enterprise in a largely secular setting. It is populist and morally serious, yet largely emancipated from a religious frame of reference. In the schools, morality is taught with admirable persistence; it is, however, secular moral consciousness about issues of race and equality, imported without resort to religious sanction. At the level of higher politics, governmental bodies charged with enquiry into areas of proposed action, or into the administration of existing state enterprise, pay no particular attention either to the need to include representative religious personnel or to address the issues concerned with religious considerations in mind. Day by day, small precedent by small precedent, the Christianity of this once Christian country is simply disappearing from public view. The Church's own insistence in sticking to the ancient parish system as the main staple of its evangelistic strategy is in fact locating religious belief in units which are increasingly removed from social advance. The secularisation of the culture has no special appeal in society; it is occurring not because of the intellectual sophistication of the critics of religion, nor because it is popular, nor even because the alternatives are full of allure. It is happening because Christian leaders themselves have reinterpreted their own faith in terms of secular moral enthusiasms, and are left with little to say either to the thinking classes or to the masses which is distinctive or, come to that, particularly religious.

7

Materialism

In society today racism is a sin – a secular moral sin – and atheism is not. One of the most telling signs of a secular polity is the elevation of human material need and the cultivation of human esteem above spiritual value. By this is meant spirituality in its traditional and religious sense: the relationship of the person to God. In modern society morality becomes classified according to its attendance upon human need: behaviour or practices which appear to enhance human well-being – the eradication of illness, the prevention of unwanted births, violence to others, for example – are the content of moral enquiry. The source or authority for morality is no longer sought in divine commands, or in ways of arranging human affairs so that the injunctions of transcendent beliefs may be given content. Humanity itself is the sovereign consideration, and goodness is defined in terms of whatever conduces to human welfare. It is no surprise, in such a context, that issues of race excite the most heightened sense of moral concern in liberal Western thought.

Discriminating between people on the basis of racial difference is in itself irrational; but debate in modern society has raised the ideal of race equality to a dogma which has such sacral supremacy as to amount to a practical deification of the entire human race. It is now regarded as more terrible to discriminate against another on racial grounds than it is to ignore God. Much of the outrage over racism expressed in modern Western societies, laudable though it is in itself, is detached from world realities. Most racial discrimination in the world is practised by non-white people: this has to be so on simply numerical grounds. Although there is a universal rhetoric of antipathy to racism, furthermore, it tends to be represented in the non-white world by Westernised élites. The disagreeable truth is that racism is universal; it appears to have been endemic in most societies and cultures. Like discrimination on the basis of gender, however, it is more easily vilified than eradicated; and the process of change, from the enlightenment of the mind to educational propaganda, to legal compulsion, and to eventual justice, would seem to be rather more complicated than modern activists suppose. The negative aspect of all this virtuous social engineering is the effect on human self-esteem. There is much emphasis on self-esteem in the educational programmes of schools today, and it stands in some contrast to the traditional Christian exhortation *not* to esteem oneself. Similarly, on the global racial scale, assuring all people that they are equal because all are equally human, though correct in point of biological fact, is only of good value if humanity is in itself good.

Christianity has taught that all people are equally God's children, and it was the Papacy, in the sixteenth century – in relation to the discoveries of new races in the New World – who defined that *all* humans had souls, however strange their behaviour and however removed from European cultural orthodoxies their manner of understanding. Christianity has also always taught, however, that humans are intrinsically corrupt and that they are, because of their separation from God, in a state of sinfulness. Sinful creatures are not admirable – and they are certainly not worthy of esteem, their own or somebody else's. Humans of all races are equal because God made them so; in the Christian world they are treated equally because the love of God for his creatures is reflected in the love of people for one another. Equality does not derive from rights, but from love: that is the Christian way. Unhappily modern movements for racial equality are necessarily involved with rights because rights are guaranteed through resort to law. Yet there is much in the New Testament about the supremacy of the practice of love over moral legalism, and Christians are constantly to be vigilant in their use of compulsion to secure righteous ends. In actual society, of course, moral virtue is embodied in legal requirements at every juncture, and Christians will be, if they are loyal to the calling of Christ, constantly concerned to promote equality among people.

This is equality as attached to those who are created and loved by God: it is not to be confused with cultural or with religious equality. There are all kinds of reasons why some ideas and practices are to be preferred to others, from the point of moral virtue. Cultural relativism is not a part of racial equality, although clarity in such matters is obscured by the unavoidable mixture of culture and ethnicity in traditional societies. In the nineteenth century liberal European colonialists were often preoccupied with the question of how long a 'native' people should be governed paternalistically, before they had been sufficiently raised in what contemporaries thought of as 'the scale of civilisation' and so could once again govern themselves. Such ideas were in general about cultural rather than racial inferiority, and they were expressed with a confidence which has departed from the world. Christians love all of God's children because he does. It is as simple as that, and God loves his people *in spite* of their sinfulness. He does not love them because he 'esteems' them. The danger inherent in the dogma of race equality in our day is precisely that it is secular. Divorced from the divine pity, the equal treatment of people is now promoted because they are believed to have virtues derived from their humanity.

In identifying itself so completely with the ideals of modern race equality, the Church is endorsing a world-picture of human moral autonomy which is at variance with the essential conviction that men and women stand in need, in the first priority, not of equality but of divine forgiveness. In practical matters Christians are called to assist racial equality, yet theirs are rather different purposes from those of the secular Humanists. They seek the promotion of God's love; the Humanists are concerned with human mutual esteem. The motivation of one is religious, and the other secular. The danger for Christians is that in furthering a good cause they will inadvertently absorb the secular ethicism of the Humanists. This already frequently occurs, indeed, as reference to the vocabulary and images employed by Christian activists in race issues will confirm. It is not because people are so wonderful that they must be treated equally, however; they are not wonderful at all. Divorced from submission to God, and bereft of a sense of human worthlessness, issues of race have become an extremely effective means of elevating humanity to a status which both practically and ideologically usurps the divine sovereignty.

There is a moral consensus in modern society about the priority which should be accorded to human material welfare. While always seeking to fulfil the love of God taught by Christ in attending to the well-being of others, however, the priority for Christians has been spiritual rather than material. Here, once again, modern attitudes now place them in a position where their acceptance of current moral objectives unavoidably involves danger for their spiritual priorities. For in seeking to attend to human material welfare, as practised in the organised circumstances of the modern collectivist state, Christians are liable to imbibe Humanist attitudes not only in the priority of the material but also in the supreme value attached to human life. It is God, Christians believe, who has supreme values, not mere men and women. In serving the needs of humanity, in the alleviation of suffering and in ordinary acts of welfare, it is

Christ who is served. But the salvation of the individual soul is more important than human welfare, and Christ is first served by submission to him.

The matter is complicated. For the salvation of the individual is related to the service of humanity: modern Christians, however, in accepting too much of the Humanist world-view, tend to regard the performance of material welfare as in itself a religious act. In traditional Christianity, on the contrary, acts of mercy and good works merely give content to the life of salvation – which is about admission of individual sin, submission to God, and a personal life at whose centre is devotional proximity to God. Modern moral culture, on the other hand, is entirely concerned with human material welfare, and to that extent excludes God: 'Except the Lord build the house: their labour is but lost that build it' (Psalm 127). Put quite simply, all the warnings that Jesus gave in his parables about the spiritual person becoming choked by earthly concerns apply exactly to modern moral concerns about human welfare. The end of the programmes of the relief of suffering, the improvements in social conditions, the eradication of sickness and bodily malfunction, is not in question; the priority of human welfare over devotion to God is.

Time and time again, however, people today are encouraged to lay aside their religious differences – often depicted as merely 'sectarian' – in order to attend to human need. Having privatised religion, and in practice having removed most symbols of observance of God from public life, religion itself is now coming to be regarded as so marginal to serious moral purpose as to be set aside in the higher interests of human welfare. Thus the application of this set of attitudes in, for example, Northern Ireland. English politicians and observers are so secularised themselves that they cannot understand a society which still retains some spiritual priorities. When they encounter them, in fact, the politicians simplistically characterise them as 'sectarian'. What they seek, instead, is a society in Northern Ireland which relegates religion to privatised observances, just like their own, and which ceases from involving religion with the conduct of public affairs. But looked at from the other side of the water, however, what the Catholics and Protestants of Northern Ireland are attempting to do, and have attempted to do for centuries, is to implement their religious teachings in the real world of public affairs. They are, that is to say, models of what the radical theologians of the 1960s were always calling for: the political involvement of the Gospel. The consequence, as is inevitably the case in a world of competing ideologies, is social division. Similarly in Islamic fundamentalism; here, too, Western observers are horrified at the policies of people who really do take their religion seriously. The results, doubtless, both in Northern Ireland and in the Middle East (and also, as is unfolding in our day, in Islamic territories of the Balkans) are less than agreeable to the Western liberal mind. But in point of principle the peoples of Northern Ireland and of the Islamic lands are correct: the service of God, as understood, has a priority over mere human need. And the two cannot simply be conflated, because everyone differs about what both concepts mean. The simple Humanist, Western, liberal, secular solution – to serve human need and to ignore religion altogether – has about it a certain grotesque crudity. It also attracts the moral sense of the educated opinion of the times.

There is also, as noticed before, a self-deception in the diagnosis of the Humanists. Their declared intention is simply to attend to material welfare and to ignore ideological justification. Human need, they suppose, is plainly evident and does not require explanation. But in practice, of course, the motivation of Humanism is itself deeply ideological, projecting, as it does, a materialist view of humanity. The finer aspects of human culture, from the Greek Sophists to the present, were

always concerned with intellectual, spiritual and moral ends
for human life which were not concerned with mere material
welfare. Our modern contention for the priority of the
material is gross by comparison; our renunciation of ideology
because it proves divisive is a betrayal of the moral past of
our culture. Christians, of all people, should not be so insensitive to their own spiritual priorities as to allow themselves
to exchange a sophisticated appreciation of the subtleties and
ambiguities of the spiritual life for the one-dimensional
materialism of the secular Humanists. They do not see it in
this manner, however. It becomes very clear from modern
Christian discourse, and from the statements of Christian
bodies, that the welfare materialism of the age is recognised
as simply an implementation of the love of neighbour
enjoined by Christ. This is the context in which 'spirituality'
becomes a process of self-exploration to discover inherent
human richness, rather than self-evaluation to discover the
depth of human corruption and the expansiveness of God's
mercy. Everything seems turned on its head: the material has
become the spiritual, and the acknowledgement of God has
become attendance to material welfare. And it is modern
Christians themselves who are proving to be most adept at
acclaiming their successor and replacement as an authentic
version of their own message.

8

Theology

There has also been a secularisation of theological understanding. The Church has always been visited by differences
of view about even the most fundamental doctrines and
teachings. The doctrine of the Church itself, indeed, has
produced divergences of theological opinion so severe as to
have provoked the major schisms within the historic Church
and the phenomenon of 'denominationalism' within Protestantism. In the English churches of the present day, however,
differences of the past, though they persist, are enormously
overshadowed by the contrast between those who adhere,
still, to 'traditional' interpretations of doctrinal formulae,
who understand Christianity as a fixed body of structured
teaching, and those 'liberal' clerics and thinkers for whom
religious faith has become a virtually open-ended exploration
of human responses to intimations of a divine purpose in
existence. Inside the Church of England there is a paradox:
recent decades have seen episcopal leadership pass into the
control of the Evangelical majority, who broadly adhere to
traditionally conceived formulations, though with biblical
rather than ecclesiological guidelines, while the liberal
minority have successfully retained the influence they have
possessed since at least the 1960s in educational work, in the
specialised ministries, and in the central offices of the
Church. Theological understanding, as exercised in educational and academic institutions, is very decidedly liberal.

The Catholic wing of the Church of England, wounded and diminished in influence by defeat on the question of the ordination of women to the priesthood, are adherents of traditional doctrine-based Christianity. With the possibility of the Church deciding to proceed to the consecration of women bishops, the influence of the Catholic wing seems likely to recede still further. The chief guardians of historic doctrinal integrity in the Church of England therefore seem to be destined for a future of continuing decline.

The secularisation of theology may perhaps accurately be characterised as acceptance of the general methods of modern intellectual enquiry, and acceptance also of the conclusions of Humanist ethics. The first of these is familiar and in a sense necessary: the Church has always encouraged and promoted intellectual enquiry, and it was indeed in Christian educational institutions that the foundations of modern liberal thinking were established. The truth of Christianity will be enhanced, and not subverted, by intellectual enquiry, since authentic knowledge amplifies human understanding of the creation and its workings as ordained by God. Interpretation of the data, however, needs to be informed by values which often derive from intellectual attitudes, and traditions of understanding, to which religion brings unique insights. When this is left out of the processes of comprehension the result is, as in present circumstances, the secularisation of analysis and explanation. Sometimes it is simply because the secular modes of intellectual enquiry are inappropriate when applied to data which derives from Revealed Truth. More commonly, however, theological interpretation proceeds by removing aspects of traditional religious belief – in miraculous phenomena, for example, or in the intrinsic corruption of human nature – which is considered by modern intellectual culture to be implausible or literally incredible. Theological 'reductionism' of this sort is no new feature: it has been evident for the past two centuries. When extended fully, the only parts of Christianity which escape elimination are the ethicist parts. Then Christ is represented as a moral teacher, and the Christian religion as a nexus of human decencies expressed in the dated vocabulary of mysterious symbolism. The most rigorous of the theological understandings which are indebted to modern secular analysis envisage the miraculous occurrences of the Bible as symbolical images and the principal events of the life of Christ as explicable in material terms – including the Virgin birth and the resurrection itself.

The second feature of secularisation, the acceptance of Humanist ethics, is a greater danger to historic faith since it is less readily recognised and more easily mistaken for a friend rather than a foe of Christianity. So great is the modern prevalence of benign views of human nature, and so insistent is the declamation of human virtue, that Christians tend to accept them at face value and merely try to add their faith as a kind of layer or dimension of it.

It is perhaps most helpful to illustrate this phenomenon. The rise of universalism is a good case to take. Christianity has always followed Christ in insisting on the division of humanity into those who will be received into eternity at the final judgement and those who, having failed to repent of their sins, will not. It is a fundamental division of the human race, and there can be no convincing form of words by which its severity can be abridged or mitigated. Jesus himself said more about judgement in his parables than about any other matter of faith: the times were evil, he told his hearers, and their lives were in need of radical amendment. In modern ethical culture, in contrast, it is offensive to discriminate with people, an affront to suggest that those without correct religious responses will be held to account, let alone to suffer eternal exclusion. Modern thought esteems human worth. Large numbers of Christians today – probably a majority, and certainly an overwhelming majority of theologians and Christian educationalists – have come to accept the

Humanist view. They, too, cannot stomach the idea of judgement, of divine discrimination in the matter of human worth. And so the whole concept, once so central, has quietly slipped out of received interpretation of the faith. Sermons are no longer preached on judgement, people no longer live in terror of hell. There is a bland and general assumption that somehow everyone will be saved; modern church leaders no longer envisage a world-picture in which vast numbers of humans are eventually to be classified as unworthy. This extraordinary change amounts to a dramatic secularisation at the very centre of Christian understanding of the purpose of life.

For the change does not derive from any re-appraisal of biblical texts but from a simple acceptance of the Humanist view of human value. In traditionally understood Christianity the concept of eternal life is about the quality of life in the world – it is a life which discloses qualities which are durable (or eternal) because they attempt to embody the commands of God and their application in the service of others. These qualities are first encountered, however, not in an acceptance of human value but in the admission of personal sin. This leads to surrender to the sovereignty of God, and then to the persistent cultivation of spiritual formation. It is this last pursuit which necessarily involves the love of neighbour, the social application, as a sign that the faith of the individual is receiving content in the world of immediate experience. First, love of God; second, love of neighbour. Since modern Humanism has eliminated the first part of this formula, in various degrees of self-consciousness, Humanist ethical idealism becomes a highly unsatisfactory basis for Christian service. Indeed its reliance on a species of calculated hedonism for its authority or effectiveness, and its appeal to merely human virtues, makes Humanist morality an enemy of religious faith since it projects wholly secular alternatives, and in the process elevates human need above divine service.

Much theological thinking of the present day, however, can cope with this because it envisages a multiplicity of approaches to a knowledge of the divine. In place of Christianity as a fixed structure of doctrinal formulation it posits a maturing humanity, progressively conscious of a material universe whose operations, though perhaps ultimately derived from a non-material Being, appear to be discoverable by men and women without any special recourse to religious tradition. Others believe that a knowledge of God may be legitimately constructed from a sympathetic appraisal of *all* religious traditions. Still others would broaden that to include all ethical systems as well – or, at least, those compatible with Western liberalism. The hazard to traditional understandings of the faith in these attitudes does not originate in their generosity with cultural data, or in scientifically verifiable knowledge, but in their refusal to accept the authority of unique revelation. Christianity has always regarded the phenomenon of Natural Religion as a proper way of perceiving the existence of the Creator. God is seen in the evidence of his works, and the various religious traditions of humanity express valid but partial interpretations of the divine intimations. The emphasis here must be on *partial*; these are fragmentary appreciations of a unitary Being, as interpreted through the distorting effects of local and cultural expectations.

Is anyone possessed of a complete knowledge of the divine? Christians believe that Natural Religion is a foundation for authentic religious truth, but that it is inactive truth – descriptions of the created order, not conveyances of divine graces. God is universal and beyond description: to be known about the universal Being needs to be particularised. Since men and women can only know things in wholly terrestrial images and values, then God needs to become one of them in order to activate a knowledge of himself. Since men and women, at an early stage in their growth in self-consciousness, came to claim exemption from their status as created beings, and to have sought, in effect, an equality with God – a practical release from suffering and deprivation – their 'Fall' (to use religious language) additionally needed a corrective. Hence the Christian doctrine of the Incarnation: the universal particularised himself, God became a man in Christ; and a fallen humanity was offered forgiveness. This act of supreme divine mercy, and the teaching of Jesus himself while in the world, constitute the main substance of Revealed Truth. This is a body of unique knowledge, and is superior to all other traditions of understanding, religious or secular, since it was introduced to the world by God himself for the explicit purpose of disclosing his will. Thus he confirmed the primitive human intimations of his existence and works, and thus his will for us may be known with certainty. And thus, in consequence, Christianity has always been expressed as a fixed structure of doctrine. It was at first taught by Christ to a distinct body of followers, whom he despatched to be evangelists in the country towns and villages of his day: it was Christ himself who founded the Church. It was at early gatherings of his greater following, the first Councils, that his teaching was arranged in systematic formulations. His body in the world, that is to say, continued to disclose his message after his actual human body – crucified, risen, and glorified – had ascended to 'the heavens'. Of this celestial realm Christians can claim little knowledge, for none of the categories of reality available to them – which refer only to the created material universe – are applicable to another state of things.

The contrast between Christianity as the guardian of this body of Revealed Truth, and Christianity conceived as open-ended enquiry, is a very great one. Though it may be bridged at certain junctures – in acknowledging the insights, even of limited utility, both of other religious experience and of secular ethical maxims – there is a fundamental antipathy between the two interpretations. If the (largely Catholic) notion of Development in religion is true, then the doctrine fixed for ever in traditional Christian understanding may be added to with the progressive recognition of unfolding dimensions of the faith. But no doctrines once proclaimed can be altered – though their applications in moral teaching may experience variations over time as knowledge of the mechanics of reality expands. In liberal Christianity (or however modern understanding of open-ended faith is to be described), on the other hand, adherents are set upon a quest for meaning whose data is universal and whose absence of exclusivity eventually projects a generalised understanding of the divine nature. Indeed, the wider the incorporation of divergent cultural insights, from the various traditions of humanity, and the more precise the inclusion of modern intellectual advance, the greater the generalising becomes. Hence the appeal of Humanist ethicism: religious faith, centred on humanity and its needs, can reinvent itself with each successive generation of enthusiasm for humanity. Stripped of the exact knowledge supplied by Revealed Truth, and dependent for its content on Natural Truth, 'liberal' Christian understanding has no clear message to contrast with modern secular Humanism. It is a kind of halfway house to what the Victorian pioneers of Freethinking would have recognised at once as fundamentalist atheism. Here is a version of religion dependent on human moral understanding, and which has no authority beyond human sentiment.

Fifty years ago disbelief in the miraculous occurrences of the life of Christ was comparatively rare among the clergy; it was a daring speculation of a minority of academic Modernists, an intellectual foible pardonable because it was capable of being judged eccentric. Now it is really only among the Evangelicals and the depleted Catholic wing that a reasonable certainty exists that the reality of, for example, the Resurrection or the Ascension, will be taught. And that is not overwhelmingly helpful when it comes to persuading educated opinion of the truth of Christianity since the Evangelicals' biblical fundamentalism, and their characteristic insistence on attributing divine causation to trivial daily incidents, detracts from their authority. In the non-Evangelical sections of the Church, and especially among the clergy engaged in educational work, the miraculous events of the life of Christ are now almost conventionally explained as symbolical tableaux. Thus the Resurrection was not a corporeal, historical event, but the experience of the continuing appeal of the personality of Jesus among Christ's followers after his death; the Ascension was a fanciful depiction in words of the glory that could be attached to the majesty of Christ. In these ways the scepticism about religious evidences found within modern intellectual culture has extended itself to the teachers of the Church, and uniquely important dimensions of the truth of Christ are diminished by being represented in wholly human terms.

Allow the matter to be stated again, for it is of supreme importance. Although it is true that all we can know about reality is derived from our observation and constructive reflection about the material creation – about the world, and the perspectives it affords – it is also true that human knowledge of the natural order has produced remarkable consistencies throughout very different cultures. There is nothing in itself mysterious about this, but it does provide a sufficiently even foundation for human knowledge as to have been categorised into a series of laws – 'Natural Laws'. Many of these, if not all of them, could well be useful fictions, and they certainly lack sanctions unless the will of human agency imposes some by acts of organised society. The point, however, is that a knowledge of a divine purpose in the Creation, the idea of a Creator, of God, is universally distributed. The Natural Religion which results from this is, as already indicated, merely descriptive: it describes human reflection on sensations derived from human perceptions about material data. It is still of the world, and is rendered in verbal images which relate wholly to the experience of the world.

Both in order to render these intimations active, and to discover which of their conflicting claims are to be considered authoritative, it is necessary for God to make a direct revelation of himself. In the Judaic–Christian tradition this revelation was prepared over a prolonged period by the religious education of a particular people, chosen by God for the purpose – making the general known through the particular – and was then confirmed and activated in the entry of Christ into the world. That entry, that decisive re-direction of information about the will of God, was by its nature and of necessity miraculous. God had made the entire universe to operate according to material laws he had established, together with their developments and variations, and human knowledge operates within them. So does life on earth. But without another world to stand upon there is no way of moving this one; without a miraculous intervention in the means by which men and women can know God there can never have been certainty that the universal intimations of his presence, and all their cultural reflections, were anything other than the inventions of humanity. The Incarnation was of necessity a miraculous event. God did not 'adopt' a human person to reveal his message, and the man Jesus was not just a genius as a religious teacher. The truth of the Incarnation is in essence miraculous: Jesus was God, in the flesh of the human creation, born to a woman but conceived without human agency, risen from the dead in his actual body, received into the celestial realms, yet with men and women still – through his earthly body, the Church, and beneath the forms of bread and wine in the miracle of sacramental grace.

It may be that 'ecclesiastical' miracles are pious folk-inventions, or mistaken ascription to divine causation by peoples living in cultures in which popular miracles were conventionally expected. It may even be that miraculous explanations were wrongly attributed by common piety to events in the Bible which were not in themselves mysterious. But the central events of the life of Christ – and doubtless also some events in the traditions of his continuing body in the world, the Church – are of necessity miraculous. For this is the essential way of authenticating the religious ideas derived from Natural Religion, and of securing salvation (activating them, that is to say) for men and women. Revealed Truth validates the perceptions of the natural order and raises human understanding to a more precise knowledge of God's commands. At the centre of Christianity are miraculous occurrences which are utterly indispensable, for they provide an entry for humans into 'eternal life' in a manner unavailable in the world of Natural Truth. Good and virtuous people before Christ had the promise, as the Letter to the Hebrews spells out, but they did not receive the fullness of Revealed Truth. Modern preachers or teachers who are sceptical of miraculous events in the life of Christ rob the religion they seek to serve of its authority – for Revelation is the bridge between time and eternity, the window on another world. In this sense, if in no other, secularised understandings of Christianity destroy the faith from within.

9

Morality

Christianity has always taught that mastery of the body, the control of human appetites and passions, is an essential part of the religious life. This is because of the beneficial effects produced both in the spiritual formation of the person and in social intercourse. Christ himself inherited a Jewish tradition of moral teaching which assumed these truths, and transmitted them in an enhanced manner to his own followers. Nearly two millennia of moral theology have examined and re-examined an accumulating mass of Christian teaching – often in a detail that seems unnecessarily precise to modern understanding. There have always been disagreements among believers themselves about aspects of Christian moral application: probably as much has been written, for example, about the moral effects of greed in eating as has been written about the sexual appetites, and the writers have differed extensively about issues of degree in calculating moral value. This particular example still has relevance in the Developing World; in Western societies indulgence in food, where it is at the present time made available in plentiful amounts, does not attract moral commentary: it is, on the contrary, an insight into the materialism of the age that it is the baneful health effects of over-eating, rather than the spiritual effects, which excite interest and concern. In most areas of moral discourse Christianity has shown great consistency throughout its history, at least in moral issues relating to mastery of the body. In social and economic morality there have been frequent reinterpretations of Christian application. Who now, for example, enjoins the prohibition of usury which existed at the centre of Christian economic morality for a thousand years? And nobody, surely, will today seriously recommend that the Church teaches the moral duty of subordination to social superiors. But in questions affecting mastery of the body there has been very little radical reinterpretation: humanity has not been very inventive at discovering new ways of committing sin.

Large areas of this collection of moral teaching are concerned with sexual morality. This is not, as some modern commentators would seek to insist, because the Church had a distaste for sexual passion founded in guilt, or because it desired to control human emotions because of prurient suspicion, but more simply because stewardship of the body and emotions of another, which is what is essentially involved in sexual relations, is among the most common of the forms in which individuals have to make moral choices. It is also a key issue in the practice of materialism: whether individuals regard their body and its impulses as a utility and the vehicle of pleasure, or whether they regard the experiences of life as occasions to realise higher purposes in existence. This is not to suggest a quasi-dualism. Body and soul are interrelated, and the one informs the other in spiritual consciousness and growth. But the passions of the flesh have an urgent persistence which easily achieves a monopoly of an individual's priorities, as moralists have always pointed out, and wisdom subsists in controlling them. Hence the Christian idea, which echoes preceding Jewish and Greek thinking, that the body is a temple of the soul.

Modern society, in some contrast, is rapidly coming to assume a quite different assessment. The pursuit of pleasure as an acceptable end for human life is combining with a

materialist understanding of the nature of men and women –
modern Humanism – to exclude the spiritual culture of self-
denial with which Christianity had once infused the
operation of personal relationships. As in the case of eating
habits, the limits are now set not by concerns about spiritual
formation but by worries about health. Sexual acts, and the
circumstances in which they are experienced, are evaluated
according to their capability to transmit disease or to inter-
fere with the supposed stability either of a particular liaison
or of a family unit. The latter is sometimes represented in
pseudo-moral categories, in which the assumption is made
that children are more satisfactorily reared in 'stable' family
environments. Despite the statistical basis for this assumption, which itself has too many variable explanations to be
conclusively convincing, the fact is that until the current
model of a stable family – largely an invention of middle-class
Western societies in the first half of the twentieth century –
very few children were actually brought up in what would
now be thought stable conditions. They were socialised exclusively by women, and they derived their sense of adulthood
from the vernacular behaviour of the streets. The great
paradox is that the stable family of modern social myth is
very fragile, with over a third of them breaking up in
divorces, whereas families in traditional societies of the past
stayed together (in extended versions) and do not appear to
have produced, as a consequence, any particularly salient
features indicating stability of temperament among the
young reared in them.

The whole matter of sexuality being related to the shape of
family living, however, has been marginalised in modern
society by the practical separation of sexual behaviour from
marriage. Despite the rhetoric of 'caring relationships' and
the need for stable families, with which the young are presented at school and in the all available means of social
propaganda, these objectives are not linked to a defined

ethical code. Children in most schools, that is to say, are not taught to seek 'caring' sexual arrangements because they are Christian but because they are socially and personally conducive – they promote the happiness of individuals and, inside families, assist the stability of the domestic environment in which children are to be reared. Their moral basis is pragmatic and their practical effects are intended to secure personal pleasure rather than the cultivation of a higher understanding of the purposes of human life.

How, then, do the churches in modern England teach sexual morality, and with what degree of priority do they regard sexual ethics within their general presentation of the Christian life? There is, at once, a contrast. The Roman Catholic Church is more obviously loyal to traditional teaching, and it is the pronouncements of the leaders, in giving public rulings to its own adherents, as also in addressing society in general according to the common duties of citizenship, which are heard. There are plenty of liberal dissenters among its own membership, but it is the Catholics who are now looked to by, for example, the media, for clear statements of Christian teaching in sexual morality. So much is this the case that the public believes that it is the Catholic Church alone which prohibits abortion, whereas in fact the Anglican Church also does so – to the evident surprise of many of its own members when they become acquainted with the fact. The Church of England, sensing both that and also, doubtless, the potential for divisions among the leadership, plays very little part in organised opposition to abortion. Its opposition to abortion, indeed, has now become rather formal: when does it criticise the training of nurses in abortion techniques in Voluntary Colleges conducted under its auspices, or when does it insist that abortion is condemned in the moral teaching given in Church Schools? The English Roman Catholic Church, united in a universal Church with a single teaching on human sexuality, appears to the public as the only one with a consistent and authoritative body of teaching in such matters. The Church of England, comparably, condemns divorce, yet increasing numbers of its clergy are resorting to divorce themselves, and the leadership is at present seeking a device whereby divorced persons may be re-married by the Church. Despite the efforts of some Evangelicals in the Church of England, who persist in condemning sexual acts outside the marriage bond, the general tenor of the Anglican clergy is to close their eyes to conduct, among their own Church members, which is now so common as to have achieved social respectability. 'Partnerships' seem routinely acceptable to them: how many sermons are now heard which give any outline guidance in issues of sexual purity or sexual commission? All manner of sexual practices which were once regarded as utterly unacceptable to Christian moralists, and which are still formally disapproved as examples of fornication, now pass without remark in the moral advice given by the clergy today. Their moral teaching on human sexuality, indeed, parallels that of the secular Humanists. Its basis is the cultivation of 'caring relationships', its test of acceptability for sexual acts is their propensity to heighten human sensibilities and to give pleasure, and its agency in the promotion of spirituality is expressed in such generalised language as to indicate a kind of spaced-out hedonism. The clergy seem terrified of seeming old-fashioned, of offending 'political correctness' – among whose otherwise rather puritanical canons is a disposition to sexual diversity.

There is a complicating dimension to this, however. Christianity has always maintained that doctrines are unchangeable: statements, that is to say, about the nature of God and the wretchedness of humanity. Doctrines may be *expressed* in different symbols through time, or in ways appropriate to differing cultures. Yet they are always, in themselves, the same. Christian morality, too, is unchanging;

yet each age and place needs to re-examine how moral teaching is to be *applied*. And the process of application may well reveal new aspects of moral law, and ways of clearing away past misunderstandings about previous applications. The question of homosexuality is a case in point today. The Church has always condemned same-sex physical relationships or sexual acts, despite the fact that many Christians have themselves been homosexual. The phenomenon of homosexuality was itself regarded as an intrinsically disordered condition – not only in Christianity, but by large numbers of religions and cultures. It is becoming plain to the modern world, however, that this condition is one over which the individual has no choice: it is either inherited as a characteristic or it is due to early conditioning over which the child has no control. That does not affect its moral status; it may well, on the other hand, indicate situations in which involuntary sexual impulses can be legitimately exercised, once it is recognised that the intentions of the person involved are not in themselves evil or depraved. In such a reconsideration of Christian morality it would first be necessary to ask if what was being condemned in the past was not homosexuality *per se* but sexual actions which would have attracted censure had they accompanied conventionally acceptable sexuality. Then it would have been sexual excess, or depravity, which were the faults, and not the inherent instincts of the individual. Heterosexual commission of a comparable nature would be equally liable to condemnation. What is needed in such an exercise of reappraisal, however, is an authoritative teaching office, or centre of authority, in the Church concerned. It cannot be left to private judgement or mere opinion, since the Church, as the body of Christ in the world, has to teach what is universally recognised as Christian truth. Where one section of Christendom acts unilaterally in such matters, or where one group in a local Christian society does so, there will inevitably be scandal and division. The Church is the body of Christ, not a debating society.

Modern England represents just such a case in point. Here the reluctance of the leadership of the Protestant Churches, and especially of the National Church, to declare its sexual morality in a coherent manner, has led to a situation in which every church member, and vast numbers of the clergy, feel themselves qualified to define morality for themselves. Their terms of reference in this are not provided by the large treasury of traditional Moral Theology, or by a resort to official teaching, but by a compilation of attitudes derived from the current presentation of moral issues in media and television debate. This is a secular frame of reference, and the moral categories from which the individual makes a personal selection are inevitably Humanist. They are also materialist, since the centre of Humanist moral judgement is the degree to which sexual action affects the pleasure or welfare of others. There is no consideration of resort to the permanent laws of Revealed Religion – the laws of God. The days have now slipped away when the producers of television discussions on issues of sexual morality included a bishop or a theologian. Doubtless they found the church dignitaries had nothing particularly distinctive to say, and the general decline of the significance of Christianity in this society of 'plural values' anyway disinclines the media to allow preference to religious leaders.

Revisionism in the application of Christian moral teaching is more appropriate in some areas than in others. Homosexuality represents a clear case, especially since the personal lives of many homosexual Christians have persistently produced evidence of authentic spirituality. But adultery is always adultery, and the circumstances in which it occurs does not alter its sinfulness. Christian moral teaching has to be divided into categories calculated according to suitability for reconsideration. Christian moral teaching itself – let it be

repeated – does not change. This exercise is about understanding its application in differing circumstances.

There is little prospect that, in the immediate future, the
clergy will stop their present practice of defining morality
individually, or that the lay members of the Church will
re-submit to ecclesiastical authority in moral law – and surrender their right, as they often see it, to define morality for
themselves. This breakdown of the perceived need for authority in the Church, the individualising of core Christian
teaching, and the secular origin of most of the data from
which modern Christian believers draw the moral ideas they
are disposed to consider acceptable, conspire together to
project a bleak future for much coherence or distinctiveness
in the Church's message.

10

Realism

People today have a problem coping with suffering and death in a way unknown to their predecessors. It indicates, in its effects, how unrealistic are modern expectations to a painless existence, and how their exalted view of humanity involves them in a false sense of what life can deliver. Christians have always recognised the material inseparability of humanity from the rest of the Creation – who have, accordingly, no claims to exemption from the natural processes of decay and bodily dissolution or from the incidence of disaster and catastrophe. Men and women, in the Christian understanding of the world, are called by God to take part in the development of the earth, but they remain integrated with it, and with the fate of all living things. They are, in the biblical image, dust. Their fate is suffering because they harbour a self-induced overestimate of their deserts: they think too highly of themselves and expect that the inevitable occurrence of earthly processes will somehow not apply to them.

With each step in the advance of knowledge, and with each development of techniques which palliate human suffering – both in medicine, and in the control of the environment – the expectations of exemption from the common fate of living things is extended upwards. It is part of the divine gift of reason and reflection that men and women should be capable of envisaging a more perfect way for human life, but their knowledge has outstripped their wisdom, and their unrealistic hope of a completely painless existence is always going to be frustrated. Nor is it, in itself, desirable: pain is the sanction which recalls people to their true natures, and which, faced realistically, can promote the highest expressions of nobility and service. A simple balance is needed in each person, between the God-given capability of advancing knowledge which may assist humanity, and the acceptance that as created beings men and women will always experience the suffering caused by the everlasting mismatch between their claims and what is available. Christians believe that the designs of Providence supply the basic terms of reference within which life on earth operates, and that the enlightenment of the mind offers the opportunity of serving God's will by attending, both individually and collectively, to the suffering of others. What Christians do not do – and what modern society now does all the time – is to complain that the world is at fault. The world, as created by God, is perfect for his purposes, and therefore for ours. Human engagement with it is a sequence of fruitful discoveries: what is discovered, rightly evaluated, is the evidence of the divine scheme. But humans are never going to lose the essential characteristics of their humanity. They are an integral part of the mass of living things which exist on the surface of the planet, and the terms of their material lives, as provided by the Creator, are set by the common laws of matter which affect all things.

Yet the lack of realism shown by modern people is exceedingly advanced. One of the greatest causes of scepticism about religious belief today, indeed, is that people find it difficult to accept the existence of a God who 'allows' human suffering. The only reason why they imagine humans entitled to exemption from suffering, as it happens, is human vanity: men and women are somehow so special, they suppose, and so important in the order of the Creation, that any apparent violation of their lives becomes a sort of secular blasphemy. And death itself seems an ultimate deprivation of the pursuit of happiness – which it certainly is. How can a God exist, they ask with increasing persistence, when humans are killed in earthquakes, or when children are born deformed, or when the most senseless disasters extinguish lives which seemed to have had such promise? As soon as life on earth is re-evaluated in terms of entitlements and rights, and an unrealistic scenario of human worth is allowed to set the course of expectations, then questions like these are inevitably going to obtrude. Humanism projects seemingly unlimited human worth; Christianity has emphasised the wretchedness of humanity. The greatness of God's love, in fact, is that he bothers with the lives of his creatures at all, and that his Son died for their sins is the astonishing centre of Christian understanding – and the only thing which imparts dignity to individual lives. It is not the natures of men and women which give them any value but the acts which God has done for them.

How, then, do the clergy and the leaders of the Church now confront the facts of suffering and death, and how do they reassure those who look to them that the will of Providence is done? The unhappy answer would appear to be that very many of them share the prevailing scepticism. They express agnosticism about the meaning of dreadful catastrophes; they, too, elevate human worth and cannot articulate a satisfactory explanation of how a merciful God can operate in such a manner. This is linked to their universalism, their growing inability to face up to divine judgement. At the bedside of the dying the modern priest is no longer likely to seek to elicit an act of contrition, or to remind the subject or the relatives of the wretchedness of human life and the need of God's forgiveness. Instead, in so many cases now, the priest is likely to offer only emollient expressions of the happiness to come, or even to join in the conventional conspiracy of well-meaning relatives in assisting the concealment from the dying of the actual imminence of death.

Similarly, when confronted with a railway disaster or with fatalities in a fire, or some comparable catastrophe, the clergy disclose a tempered agnosticism about the meaning of the event. The simple truth – that human life exists in an unstable environment, and that human inventiveness involves risk – is not acceptable to those who have come to claim exemption from their humanity, who claim to be too valuable to be harmed by the material processes that govern the fate of the Creation. God established the world and the universe according to real material laws, and human life exists within them and operates as they will dictate. The biblical, and therefore Christian, understanding of humanity, and of divine judgement, makes it clear that the greater part of the human population of the world has always been destined for ultimate extinction: narrow is the way, in the image of Christ himself, which leads to eternal life. This is quite unacceptable to large numbers of modern clergy – as it is to their charges. The combination of universalism, the elevation of human value, and an inability to countenance belief in a divine scheme which denies the priority of human happiness, accounts for the agnosticism of so many in the Church today when confronted with suffering. It is also an indication of their secularisation.

The same lack of realism about the actual terms of human life also now attaches to animal life. Modern people separate out non-human forms of life quite arbitrarily, regarding some creatures as comparable in sentiment and consciousness to themselves (the sort which they make domestic pets, or whose antics in television wildlife programmes seem so endearing), and some creatures as vile enemies to be destroyed on sight (spiders, for example, or the sorts of bacteria which cause illness). These attitudes began in earlier separations of urban and rural living: today even the most rural locations are actually inhabited by people with urban values – a result of mass education and electronic communication. But when people first emancipated themselves from the social deference of rural society, and sought a life in towns, their attitude to animals began that process of romanticisation which has become so advanced. Little children are now given, at the youngest age, fluffy representations of approved living things – the sort which can be imaginatively endowed with human sentiments – and taught to simulate human affection by regard for them. In the secularised moral culture, as a result, it is teddy-bears and 'cuddly' toys, rather than symbols of the cross, which are now placed on the graves of children, or are left at the scenes of tragedy.

The phenomenon is selective because the animals employed as surrogate recipients of human affection appear to be chosen largely on the basis of size and appearance. Cats and bears are especially acceptable; AIDS viruses and head-lice are not. Yet all are living creatures, and are equally with humanity created by God and have a common existence on the surface of the planet. Socialising very young children by allowing them to attribute human sentiments to animal toys creates for them a personal world of innocence which has no real existence. Their lives thereafter contain a searing attempt to discover again an idyll which was never available. What modern people cannot cope with is the idea that life is integrated: that existence subsists in the mutual absorption of living things, for sustenance and space. Urban people, long since separated from the raw materials of Creation, find this an unsatisfactory, even a primitive, scheme of things. But it is the way God has made life, and it is all that is on offer. Humanity has no exemption from this either, and in its actual treatment of animals – these days largely closed off from public view or knowledge by modern farming and distribution techniques, and comparable to popular ignorance about the nature of death – it shows no special behavioural patterns. Our romanticism about animal life, however, is irrational, and when the reality and the romantic symbols come into an unfavourable juxtaposition, the first person to get blamed for the shocking facts of existence is God.

In their attitude to animal life, therefore, as in their attitude to human life, modern men and women have set up models of reality which are at some variance from the real Creation made by God. No wonder they find it difficult to believe in his existence. There is no excuse, however, for the clergy or the leaders of Christian opinion when they, too, adopt a secular frame of reference in which to evaluate either the human or the animal creation. Animals are always to be respected, for they are God's creatures, and suffering is as real for them as it is for men and women, at least in its physical qualities. False romanticism, on the other hand, sets up unrealistic expectations of what life can deliver, and is in itself a misunderstanding of the nature of the world.

Disasters and catastrophes have a peculiarly dramatic effect in modern society because they so clearly defy human attempts to control the terms according to which life is lived. They are also sudden revelations of the impotence of men and women in the face of their own mortality, a nasty contrast to the comfortable and sanitised existence which they so insistently consider their birthright. Catastrophe suddenly discloses the real nature of things. Unable to cope, people increasingly self-dramatise their response, many plainly deriving a delicious thrill from tasting the forbidden fruit of events out of human control. Public responses to such events as crowd disasters in sports stadia, or the death of celebrities, or transport accidents, are not indicators of ordinary grief: they are emotional releases, extravaganzas of sentiment, in a world which progressively offers them little enough personal acquaintance with the horrific details of human death. For death, too, has been secularised. Its messy realities are now

handled by professionals in hospital wards; the dying themselves deprived of fully conscious participation by the
widespread use of pain-killing hallucinogenic drugs. The
occasions for religious reflection are therefore diminishing
for the dying themselves by the way in which death is now
managed – out of sight, largely divorced from the sharper
sensations of pain, unattended by rites of religion. It is a
further indication of the secularisation of social custom that
the clergy take little part in an occasion which was once their
exclusive preserve. And when they *are* present, their contribution is no longer especially distinctive – a prayer over the
dying, a word of (often quite unwarranted) consolation to the
surviving relatives.

But mass reaction to a public sensation like a railway
disaster allows each person to dramatise a response to death:
a secularised resuscitation of unremembered traditional
grief, expressed in terms of agnostic questioning about the
meaning of life. How the public then indulge themselves!
Memorial services – commemorative staged events separate
from funerals – even when organised under Christian
auspices, are often more approximate to pagan than to religious occasions. For they celebrate the merely human aspects
of the departed, usually enhanced with selections of secular
poetry or music which the dead person would have found particularly moving or pleasurable. They deliberately expunge
reference to human failings, human wretchedness, the certainty of divine judgement – and even reference to death
itself. Memorial services are in effect funerals in transition to
becoming wholly secular and ethicist. Their religious content
is becoming less and less explicit, the traditions of understanding to which they refer more and more generalised.
They are, in short, celebrations of humanity. When they are
organised for the dead in a catastrophe, or for a noted
celebrity, they become showcases for the anonymous
Humanism which, in today's society, is becoming the conven-

tional currency of emotional exchange. Surprisingly, in view of their real utility in furnishing an alternative to explicit religion, the clergy appear to find little problem in organising these events.

11

Society

In the 1960s and 1970s the English churches derived their social and political attitudes from the moral enthusiasms with which the liberal intelligentsia had infused the contemporaneous political culture, and the result was distinctively radical or at the very least progressive. There was much negative talk about the 'power structures', the need for industrial democracy, for social justice, and about the supposedly baneful ethical consequences of capitalist economics. Today the social and political teaching of the churches is less precise – as the surrounding political culture is less precise – but the process of emulating the passions of the age survives intact.

When the public life is informed or even moulded by religious ideas, as in the traditional societies of the past, the Church's engagement with it becomes a dialectical exchange; where the encompassing culture is largely secular, as in England today, however, and as in the 1960s, the effect tends to the secularisation of the Church. The Church of England, in particular, has many of the characteristics of a class institution, and its absorption of moralist idealism reflects that of the secularised middle class whose predominance in professional life, and especially in the world of education, is overwhelming. These class ideals are liberal, and are at the present time encased in the categories of political correctness. Though they are often held by individuals in a token fashion – to the extent that lifestyles are often unaffected by the simultaneous profession of political notions about equality and social justice – they are nevertheless rigorously entertained. The English bourgeoisie is divided within itself over social and political questions; the Church, however, predominantly echoes the sentiments of the articulate liberals.

In the 1960s this wing flirted with socialism and even a diluted version of Trotskyite anarchism, held in a highly romanticised way, as was the custom of the time. Students went to makeshift barricades in Maoist jackets, and the clergy spoke glowingly of the tight little Communist regime in Cuba as if it was an anticipation of the Kingdom of Heaven. Now that has all passed away – or very nearly so. What is there in the political and social idealism of the modern intelligentsia which, with a political ruling élite which makes much of 'modernisation', attracts the enthusiasm of the church leaders? There is a problem of analysis here, for the ultimate ethical ideals of the political parties in England today are not coherently expressed. Where they do receive any kind of considered statement it is in moral generalities so general as to be compatible with virtually any actual arrangement of national resources. What is absent, however, is socialism. The vulgar Marxism which was so freely spattered about in Anglican official reports and meetings of the 1960s and 1970s has all gone. Serious philosophical Marxism, which remains an authentically important intellectual tool, was little represented in the Church of the second half of the twentieth century, and is virtually extinct in it today. Once there was an intellectually respectable 'Christian–Marxist dialogue', in which the leading Christian contributors were generally Catholic academics: this, too, is now without significant influence. The Church today, reflecting the secular moral culture, as ever, is concerned with rights issues – social exclusion, race, women's equality, educational equalitarianism, and so forth. These are all classic preoccupations of the liberal bourgeoisie, and many of them are indeed desirable according to their own merits. Strikingly absent, however, are references to the existence of a class society, to irrationalities in the distribution of wealth, or to the evils of acquisitiveness.

The prosperity which has descended upon the country since the 1960s and 1970s has been a class anodyne: it is Marxism which has, alas for ideological cultivation, been relegated to the museum of antiquities. The distribution of wealth shows as many inequalities as ever – indeed the chasms have grown wider. Wealth is now populist: the modern crescendo of gambling, especially in the National Lottery, has seen to that. The bread and circuses which once had the utility of diverting the attention of the poor from the effects of their poverty are today supplied by holidays in the Costa del Sol and wall-to-wall carpeting in the living room. This is the age of vulgar materialism. Political vision equals it: the enthusiasm of parties is now represented in agenda which guarantee the fruits of popular capitalism rather than their re-distribution, and which extend the quality and availability of welfare provision in an explosion of collectivist interventionism. Both politicians, as it happens, and the Christian publicists and clergy whose priorities are in correspondence, enfold this materialist *Weltanschauung* in a veneer of social moralism, weeping, occasionally, tears of pity for the 'socially excluded', or for ethnic minorities, but leaving social greed in the driving seat of public policy.

Now there are doubtless many aspects of all this whose assessment is outside the professional competence of the Church or the clergy – just as Archbishop William Temple used to say. The balance of the economy is not the kind of thing a reasonable person would wish to see considered by the likes of the General Synod of the Church of England. Yet the personal indulgence, and the general moral culture of gain for its own sake, which describe the present mood, are very much within the area of Christian teaching, even if it is to be teaching addressed to its own members and no longer offered to the nation at large. Nowhere is the internal secularisation of the Church's message so plainly evident as in its failure to condemn the indulgent lifestyles of people in modern society. The effects of affluence are censured, indeed, only to the extent that they are harmful to health or to social welfare – no longer because of the hazards to spiritual formation. Gambling is now largely considered as morally acceptable by the Church – which would not dare to attack the popular success of the Lottery anyway. Doubts arise only over the possible detrimental consequences for domestic budgets for those who over-indulge.

The same utilitarian approach is taken by the Church over drinking: it is the health or crime effects which seem to matter, rather than the failure of those who succumb to achieve spiritual mastery over the bodily appetites. Sexual indulgence is the same. All kinds of sexual practices which were once considered evidences of personal debasement are now casually regarded as healthy expressions of pleasure. The Church of England has long ago given up theological consideration of artificial means of birth control, presuming the ethical questions involved to have been self-evidently settled. Its teaching on abortion is clear – it forbids it in all circumstances – but this teaching is rarely given public expression, and the matter seems to be considered, by the Church's leadership, as too controversial to handle. The laity consider themselves, anyway, entitled to make up their own minds. Teaching over divorce is similar. And when it comes to indulgence of the senses and bodily appetites, the most widely spread sin of the present day, the Church is very largely silent.

In the 1960s, leading Christian writers and preachers demanded structural (political, that is to say) solutions to social and moral evils: the irregularities in the lives of individuals were evidences of a wrongly ordered society, and if society was changed in the basis of its organisation the evils would disappear. There was a great deal wrong with this diagnosis, but at least it was intellectually mature. Today it is the evils themselves which are no longer regarded as evils, and the concept of the overthrow of society seems utterly inconceivable. The Church has come broadly to accept the life of materialist indulgence, and only gets into a morally directive mood when it comes to economic inequalities in the Developing World produced by the supposedly exploitative policies of the global economy, or to the cancellation of Third World debt. Who, in England, worries about the effects on the spiritual formation of the individual of demands for an ever-increasing list of material or welfare benefits? Who is concerned that bodies are treated as utilities and souls are defined in terms of mere aesthetic sensation? The socially marginalised, and those who cannot cope, are discussed in general categories, as 'welfare problems' calling for the attention of collectivist agencies. Who now teaches that the soul is educated by attending to the needs of others? Instead they urge forward social action as a species of hedonistic self-interest. People today are rapidly becoming victims of their own pursuit of material gain and their sacralising of personal welfare. When eternity no longer seems pressing as a priority in life it is bodily health and security which worry the individual, nag at the demand for security, frustrate the claim to happiness. It is the same with the fruits of affluence. People who own so much become absorbed by the preservation of their property: they are prisoners of what they own. The neurotic insecurity of this age has one of its roots here. 'Foxes have holes, the birds of the air have their nests, but the Son of Man has nowhere to lay his head'. The words of Christ demolish the false expectations of a secular redemption dependent upon a multiplication of material benefits. When does the Church speak out?

12

Authority

At the centre of the problem of secularisation, and the reason why its effects on the Church are now so dire, is the coincidence of an imprecise definition of authority within the English Protestant tradition and the modern individualising of religious choice. Ecclesiology, or the Doctrine of the Church itself, is about the manner in which Christianity is known to be true – it is about authority, and it is differences of view about this matter which have accounted for most of the historic divisions within Christendom. Christ himself founded the Church, when he selected the 12 and then sent out the 70 others to proclaim his salvific news: he established a means of transmitting his truth, that is to say, and committed the message not to a philosophical system, or even to written texts, but to an organic agency, a living body of people, the 'People of God', the Church. It is this people who still today constitutes his body in the world, and it is this people who originally, after two centuries, drew up the canon of Sacred Scripture as a record and a set of proofs of the Christian Revelation.

This body authenticated its teaching through the *magisterium*, the teaching office of the Church; what the world calls 'Christianity' is actually what this people declares when it acts universally and within its own apostolic tradition. There was, however, never a time when either the precise constitution of the body, or its understanding of its message, was uncontroverted; even the letters included in the New Testament show evidences of differences, often sharply held, among the earliest believers. The crucial question – how is Christian truth known to be true? – still divides those who call themselves Christian, and although the lack of extensive knowledge of their own beliefs which now characterises modern Christians renders many aspects of division ideologically opaque, the persistence of division derives from one crucial incompatibility.

In the Orthodox and Latin Catholic understanding of the Doctrine of the Church there exists an infallible teaching office: authentic Christian truth exists where adherents proclaim truths which are determined by reference to a universal gathering of the Church – in a General Council – and where individual believers are loyal to teachings which are accepted universally. There can be no such thing as a 'national' Church, only local and cultural variations which reflect the need for more immediate expression of ideas which are nonetheless universally acclaimed. Truth is defined in relation to central doctrines and moral disciplines, and those are unchanging; a larger number of both specific and general *applications*, which may change with time and circumstance, are re-defined periodically over the centuries. All doctrines, once determined, are equally true but are arranged in a hierarchy of importance which may alter over time. In the Protestant Churches, in contrast, no infallible teaching office is recognised, and in sixteenth-century Europe the setting up of national churches anyway precluded the possibility of access to universal councils. Truth is determined by resort to Scripture, and points of difference in the interpretation of scriptural texts are decided by local choice.

In most modern Protestant ecclesiologies a kind of free market in theological and ecclesiastical concepts is envisaged: Christ is depicted as having conveyed his message to very many different understandings, and truth emerges over time in a series of, as it were, dialectical exchanges. It was never intended that the individual would determine Christian truth for himself in most Protestant thinking, but with the development of Evangelicalism in the last two centuries, and with the impact of modern liberalism, many Protestants today believe themselves entitled to determine scriptural interpretation without explicit reference to collective authority.

The disintegration of religious unity in the modern state – the rise of denominationalism – led to the removal of erastian political management of the Protestant Churches, except in the most residual surviving formalities, and this has considerably accelerated the decline of authority, at least in a coherent sense, in the determination of religious truth in the major Protestant confessions like the Church of England. Anglicans have Articles of Faith which preclude the possibility that General Councils of the Church can be the source of infallible teaching, and as a matter of historical practicalities, anyway, they have no access to them. Anglicans, indeed, do not appear to be possessed of a systematic Doctrine of the Church at all, having their corporate origin in a selection of sixteenth-century theological and matrimonial difficulties in which ecclesiological issues were not allowed to predominate. Presumably at the time of the English Reformation short-term exigencies seemed more pressing; public men were not aware at the time that they were setting up a new Church, in which, with the effluxion of time, questions of authority would become pressing. Erastian control disguised the accumulating problems for four centuries, and they remain essentially unaddressed to this day.

Now between the idea of the Church as founded with an indefectible teaching office, and the idea of the Church as a set of loyalties to a shared understanding of Scripture, there is a basic incompatibility. The distinction corresponds to the difference between Catholic and Protestant in modern

England. Because both still proclaim the truth of the central core doctrines – the Holy Trinity, the divinity of Christ, and all the lateral amplifications – there is an appearance of a shared orthodoxy. This 'deposit of faith', rendered unstable by the consequences of modern liberal scholarship, in both Protestant and Catholic traditions, and especially in the former, has nevertheless a kind of reality. It exists on borrowed time, however. The churches still declare their truths within the world picture supplied by extensions of the Mediterranean cultures of the ancient world – but this context shows indications of imminent disintegration. Whatever succeeds it, in the culture and learning of the new millennium, will prompt formidable problems of Christian reinterpretation. Hence the need for authority, for a coherent ecclesiology. Christian essentials will have to be rescued from the detritus of a collapsed cultural world, and rendered in the emerging images and symbols of the new. But there is another and even more immediate reason why the issue of authority – of how Christian truth is known to be true – must be determined. And that is the identification of error.

The word 'heresy' now has such pejorative resonances, and is used with such technical imprecision even by senior clergy, that it is hazardous to introduce it into analysis. The reason for a systematic ecclesiology, and for authority in the determination of doctrine and teaching, however, is as much centred in the recognition of error as it is in the positive definition of truth. Most of the essential doctrines of Christianity have, after all, long since been established: at the early Councils of the first few centuries theology formalised, and the dogmas of the faith were given systematic expression. The Church is organic – it is, in the image used by Christ himself, a growth like that of a mustard seed, from a tiny grain to a mature plant. It can, as living things do, bring forth new growths, and the Catholic tradition of Christianity has come to recognise that 'Developments' of doctrine occur: doctrines always true come to be recognised over time and emerge as ready for formal definition. Not all understandings of Christianity accept the notion of 'Development', however, and the Protestant denominations, including the Church of England, do not. Yet there is a general agreement about the other function of authority in the Church – the identification of doctrinal error, or heresy.

The problem is that because some Protestant confessions, including the Church of England, are not possessed of a coherent Doctrine of the Church they cannot, in practice, determine truth or error. The early Councils of the Church were all called in order to identify heretical ideas, but since the Reformation the Church of England has had no access either to participation in Councils or to the canonical authority of Rome. For many years, in fact, doctrine in the Church of England was determined, under the Royal Supremacy in religion, by the Judicial Committee of the Privy Council, a tribunal whose members had no requirement to be – and often were not – members of the Church. Synods determine matters of discipline and order, so the revivals of synodical government in the Church of England, since 1970, have not helped to clarify questions of doctrinal ambiguity (of which there are many) or to assist in the determination of error. Indeed, the modern Church of England, with its self-consciously liberal attitudes, finds considerable distaste with the whole idea of determining error. It is probable that any serious attempt at the imposition of unitary teaching in doctrinal matters would result in the collapse of the entire Church – it is a body, after all, which already exists in a state of practical division over the question of the acceptance of the priesthood of women. Though no one will use the words, the reality is that there are two Churches of England, with parallel sets of bishops, the one allowing the priestly ministry of women and the other not. The Church was once held together by erastian controls exercised by the Crown in

Parliament, and by loyalty to the Book of Common Prayer. Both of these have ceased to operate as cohesives in the past fifty years. The most recent Anglican arrangement for worship, the book known as *Common Worship,* embodies a culture of choice, exercised through local option, which, if anything, encourages still less uniformity. Liturgical use, therefore, is scarcely likely to supply modern Anglicans with a working *lex orandi* – a source of doctrinal authority rendered through worship.

The determination of authority remains absolutely essential if the Church is to resist error. The importance of protecting the purity of Christian teachings is as great as ever it was. Indeed, it is even more necessary to have an agreed source of authoritative teaching when the most vociferous and prestigious of the theologians often seem to signal a rejection of the notion of the Church actually having a fixed body of doctrines and teachings at all. Many now claim as an article of their own faith that what is called 'Christianity' is compatible with an enormous number of modern liberal beliefs, many of which are quite frankly secular in origin and intention. Above all, however, a means of determining error is particularly crucial when those who attend church regard it as a matter of right that their understanding of Christianity should derive, not from authority, nor from those who traditionally have declared it, but from their own selection. And modern churchgoers do expect to be able to make a personal selection, both of doctrines and teachings, of styles of worship and of moral applications of the faith.

Here may be witnessed the conjoined effects of universal education, cultural relativism, the rejection of authority in general and of authority in ideas in particular, the notion that religious worship is about personal emotional satisfaction, and the supervening dogma of choice itself. People tend no longer to recognise church membership as integration with the body of Christ in the world, and therefore as involving as a priority personal and disciplined adhesion to the teaching derived from the past, to the apostolical tradition. They see it, on the contrary, as a matter of engaging in a quest for personal significance. This is, once again, religion as therapy; its appeal to the adherent is no longer centred in a sense of duty and loyalty to God but in the degree to which it accommodates individual perceptions of 'spirituality'. Churches have become the venues for personal selection. People shop around to find places where their religious requirements can most satisfactorily be met. They make up their own menus, devising personal understandings of Christian faith which they do not feel constrained to hold in versions compatible with historic formulae. In their ethical understanding, too, modern people believe it appropriate that authority resides in their own judgement, informed by media debate and the images on the screen, and not by acceptance of religious authority. As a consequence the ethical consciousness of most people, including Christian adherents, is now becoming formed by modern secular attitudes. Church leaders, seemingly reluctant to press traditional teachings (or modern teaching indebted to traditional moral understanding) remain silent on many issues relating to, for example, sexual morality or personal lifestyles.

The coincidence at the present time of rejection of authority in religion, and the phenomenon of personal selection of religious teachings, is lethal. The Catholic Church in England is better placed in what amounts to a real crisis of authority in religion, partly because numerically it has a more substantial base from which modern decline is taking place – its own members, that is to say, have always been more systematic in observance – and partly because it is a truly universal body, whose authority is determined externally to the local irregularities which are beginning to emerge in Western countries. The Catholic Church has a clear Doctrine of the

Church, a sure means of determining authority. However much the Catholic clergy and laity may begin to adopt the liberal attitudes of the encompassing moral culture around them, there remains still – but for how long? – the restraining hand of Rome. For the Protestants, and for the Church of England, something that is beginning to have the appearance of a melt-down is occurring. With no coherent ecclesiology, no means of identifying error or of defining doctrine except the judgements of individuals, and with no external authority, the English Protestant churches are especially open to all kinds of erroneous ideas.

The Church of England is particularly liable to error. For so long related to the transient enthusiasms and idealism of the governing élites, it now finds itself socially marginalised; without a clear social base; with rapidly diminishing access to the places where the decisive ingredients of the prevalent moral culture are selected; and with a ministry which is less well educated, in relative terms, to the people it seeks to address. In these conditions the absence of a means of determining its own authority is proving fearfully damaging. And yet – another Anglican paradox – the leaders of the Church of England do not appear to sense the present crisis as an ideological crisis at all. They are concerned about falling church attendance, and about a whole range of organisational matters, and about the spiritual health of the nation as a whole (in a rather imprecise way, however), but they appear unaware that the absence of a systematic teaching office is the root of all their difficulties. When an organism cannot identify its enemies it gets taken over by them. The body needs immunology. The Church needs an institutional means of determining error – or it will become, as it has already become in some measure, a victim of its ideological opponents.

What used to be called 'entryism' in Labour Party politics has long been a feature of modern Anglicanism. It cannot, as an institution, resist the adoption of alien ideas and attitudes, of false doctrine, when it does not have an immune system: a means of identifying error, a source of authority, a Doctrine of the Church itself. Where lay people are encouraged to work out religious ideas for themselves, without reference to fixed doctrinal requirements, and where the clergy are principally trained with the intention that they shall assist them in this enterprise, as they are now, all kinds of ideas enter the Church. A spiritual relativism is creeping over the entire body – it is 'spirituality' in the modern, largely secular usage of the concept – and it is coming to be regarded as the essence of Christianity. The English churches – all of them in some degree – are being infiltrated by secular ideas, and authentic adhesion to doctrine is becoming displaced by modern secular ethicism.

The Church, and especially the Church of England, has no effective means of resisting the process. Nor does it have the will to do so. It has become, indeed, a willing partner in its internal secularisation; the first to re-evaluate its core message in terms of ordinary human welfare and emotional sustenance. Its members are showing themselves apparently capable of recognising Christianity not only as wholly compatible with secular Humanism but as envisaging the Church as an embodiment of the virtues proclaimed by Humanist moral consciousness. Behold the fruits of theological liberalism: decades of reductionism and scepticism have so weakened the body that virtually anything can now enter it without serious challenge. Only those Catholics, probably still a majority of Catholics, who adhere to an indefectible teaching office, and those Evangelicals who are loyal to Scripture, seem capable of resistance to the invasion of alien ideas. Both, however, are being articulately discredited by the liberals, who are in possession of the places of learning and education and the media – and for whom Catholic 'traditionalists' represent a dying understanding of Catholicism, and for whom the Evangelicals are simply ignorant of sophisticated ideas.

Of all the causes of the present malaise of Christianity in England the absence of a coherent source of authority in the National Church, and the culture of individualising of religious belief by those patronising the churches, are the most serious. Their effects will be, accordingly, the most damaging.

13

Politics

Some will ask how it is that a nation which has a constitutional Establishment of religion should simultaneously produce so little evidence of support by public figures for Christianity. The fact, of course, is that the relationship of the Church of England to the state is now in large measure simply a constitutional formality. During the nineteenth century, in a series of *ad hoc* adjustments of the law, the official exclusivity of the Established Church was progressively dismantled. Initially this was a controversial proceeding; each step was brought forward by the agents of Protestant Dissent and each was in turn contested by the friends of the Church. By the start of the twentieth century, however, the broadening of the constitutional basis – which had its electoral counterpart in the widening of the franchise – had become generally accepted. The ancient confessional state had by then been effectively abandoned, political participation was opened to persons of all religion and of none, the legal safeguards of the Established Church had been rendered highly anomalous, as they remain to this day, and the nation had settled for the continuation of a state Church but without any of the privileges, apart from ceremonial ones, which had once adhered to it.

It is important to notice that this momentous change was the work of Christian reformers: their intention was not the weakening of the position of the Church and certainly not the promotion of secularisation. What they sought was religious equality between the denominations. The truth was that the Established Church of England, as a mid-century census of religion showed, received the adhesion of only half of the population; the Protestant Dissenting denominations, and the Catholics, could reasonably claim that their constitutional inferiority had no basis in political and social reality. This was to assume that the Establishment of religion should rest on a majority principle – a view at the time entertained by Whigs, and later argued by the Liberal Party. Conservatives continued to maintain that Establishment recognised the truth of the doctrines taught by the Church, as the spiritual arm of the nation, and need have no foundation in numerical superiority. The general decline in church attendance came to render the latter position increasingly less convincing to political activists and observers. During the twentieth century the links of Church and state remained surprisingly stable. Indeed, in the support of educational institutions under the auspices of the Church – whose costs are largely met by government grants – the relationship of Church and state has received enhanced significance. Yet a sign of the constitutional shift is that schools conducted by *all* religions are now eligible for public financial assistance: the State Church no longer receives exclusive privileges.

As the state has made a practical separation from the endorsement of Christianity, though without abandoning the formal constitutional link, the Established Church, for its part, has sought ecclesiastical autonomy. The twentieth century saw the abandonment by the state of most of the reality of erastianism. Parliament, by then opened up to persons of all religions, was plainly no longer qualified to be the legal governing body of the Church of England. In 1970, following earlier essays in self-government, the Church achieved a structure of synodical government. Church and state have in practice separated without a constitutional disruption, in a protracted sequence of characteristically English pragmatic adjustments. The position of the Sovereign as Supreme Governor of the Church has not really been especially significant – certainly not as significant as the press always assumes. An establishment of religion exists where there is a constitutional connection between political process and religious opinion. It may, as in the English case, involve a relationship between the state and only one Church, or it may, as England's developments have shown, embrace a relationship of support or recognition of a number of churches or other religious bodies. Nor does the Church in an exclusive Establishment have to be (as in England's case) a 'National' Church: the Catholic Church is wholly a universal institution, and yet there are numerous historical examples of it being established by law in the constitutions of individual states. Nor, also, does the position of the Crown have to be exclusive. The Sovereign is not only the first Anglican when in England; when in Scotland the Sovereign is a Presbyterian, for there the Established Church is Presbyterian. Some of the anomalies of the relationship of Church and state are of long standing.

Yet despite the formal constitutional position the political élite, the press and media, the teachers in the schools, the public institutions, do not behave as if there was an Establishment of religion. The country has rapidly advanced to a practical secularisation of both thought and self-identity. This has had very little to do with the widespread recognition that England is now a multi-ethnic society, or that it could now be said to encompass multiculturalism. For the basis of present attitudes was already in place before the mass immigrations of citizens from overseas in the mid-twentieth century. The acceptance of a practical secularisation is the work of the educated élites. It is they who have given up public support for the Church or for institutionalised Christianity. Expressed in the most general terms, the governing groups and those who formulate their ideas once employed organised Christianity as the vehicle of their moral seriousness. The (rather scant) available evidence appears to indicate that the population in general has never been visited with huge amounts of enthusiasm for religion, and most of the new churches built for them in the urban areas in the nineteenth century remained virtually unpatronised. What seems to have happened is that the governing sections underwent a mild religious renaissance in the middle years of the nineteenth century, stamped the Victorian age with their version of religious moralism, and then, very shortly after their most vigorous enterprises, gradually began to recede from Christianity. Lost habit took as much part in this as positive intellectual scepticism. By the end of the twentieth century the withdrawal of active support for institutional Christianity within the opinion-forming sections of society was conventionalised. Religion had ceased, in everything but the most insignificant ways, to express the moral seriousness of public life. Yet nothing had taken its place. It was not that there was nothing with a wide enough acceptance within the governing élites to fill the vacuum: the surprising thing is that there was no vacuum. An undeclared, unrecognised practical Humanism has since served for such justification as has been felt necessary to account for the moral enthusiasms of public life – and this had the greater utility when it became clear that the official leaders of the surviving Established Church appeared happy to employ the same rhetoric of Humanism in their broad endorsement of public policy.

There remain a few survivals of effective establishment status for the Church of England. It is possessed, still, of the ancient religious endowments of the nation – the actual cathedrals, church buildings, and associated incomes derived, as a consequence of nineteenth-century rationalisations, from the Church Commissioners, a body set up under statute law. The precedent of Irish Disestablishment in the

Act of 1869 made it clear that these properties and revenues
of the Church are owned by the public and are at the disposal
of Parliament. The Church of England also enjoys a number
of rather symbolical pre-eminences on official occasions. In
practice, however, it is becoming conventional for leaders
from all the major world religions who have representative
communities in England to take part in major national and
civic ceremonial events. The state, in this area of change, is
moving towards an inter-faith as well as an interdenomina-
tional quasi-confessionalism. The Christian churches have
Chaplains appointed in public institutions like the military
and the prison service; here, too, however, the other religious
bodies now receive recognition and a measure of state sub-
vention. There are numerous surviving traces of the former
recognition of Christianity – in the law, municipal custom, in
higher education, the presence of the bishops in the House of
Lords, and so forth – but none of these amount to significant
state sponsorship of Christianity. Comparable survivals are
found throughout American life, despite the constitutional
separations of Church and state which occurred there at both
federal and state levels.

The fact is that the realities of power are exercised without
reference to religion. Politicians do not routinely consult religious opinion when legislating even on matters (like medical
ethics or sexual law reform) of obvious concern to the Church
– or, at least, consultation is no more with the Church, considered as one among a number of interest groups, than it is
with any other body. There is no longer any effective sense in
which it can be said that Christianity is the moral conscience
of the state, or that the Church is the spiritual arm of government. Politicians, indeed, almost vie with one another in
avoiding the politically incorrect references which once were
made to the Christian religion as the basis of English society.
Thus the force and practical working of the 'plural society'.
Occasionally the press runs stories about political parties

seeking to associate themselves with Christianity, or with the 'Faith Communities', for electoral reasons, or in order to locate some authentication of what are considered 'family values'. These speculations, however, evergreen though they might appear to be, are running up against the buffers, once again, of political correctness, for they are violations of the secular vision of social pluralism.

There is in fact no way in which the survival of the Church of England as a National Establishment of religion can be considered any other than an extraordinary anomaly. The state simply does not behave as if it had any significant relationship to Christianity when it comes to actual legislative processes. The business of the nation is now conducted in a wholly secular fashion. Pronouncements of church leaders, which even twenty years ago could occasionally be arresting, are now only newsworthy if the press perceives a hint of embarrassment in them for the politicians. It is, anyway, the Cardinal Archbishop of Westminster whose words are more likely to be reported than are those of the leader of the Church of England.

Disestablishment, on the other hand, may not be a wise rationalisation of existing realities. This is not a question which should be judged in relation to the possible effects of such a policy on the Church. If the Church of England really is part of the Catholic and apostolic inheritance, as it claims, then the matter of its relation to the state, in the perspective of centuries, is of no significant consequence in assessing its prospects of survival. If, on the other hand, it is a mere parliament Church, as Catholic observers have from time to time supposed, then the long-term effects of the withdrawal of lingering erastian protection could be fatal. But that erastianism has already been removed in practice – except in the matter of property and incomes. It would be unfortunate to have to conclude that the Church of England is kept going because Establishment status provides the worldly structure which any institution needs to survive. It is the effect of Disestablishment on the *state* which is the more serious consideration. The symbolical de-consecration of the life of a nation is a grave moment in its history, a decisive act of self-evaluation which ought to be taken only after the most profound and philosophical enquiry into the basis of human association. From confessing a higher purpose for human society, even in a very residual manner, to regarding its members only as subjects of policing and material welfare, is a very serious matter. Nothing in the existing mode of public debate suggests that consideration of the Disestablishment of the Church – or even broadening the base of Establishment by further inclusions – will be any other than superficial. The constitutional recognition of the fact of secularity has logic and consistency; yet the surviving sentiments of men and women still reared in the afterglow of Christian allegiance would probably receive injury.

There is no widely accepted theoretical or symbolical alternative to the Christian religion as the justification of public moral consciousness. That is a different thing from saying that Christianity is widely believed in, or that, in a referendum, people would know their best interest. In the latter exigency the members of the public would doubtless 'think for themselves'; would be, as usual, terrified of seeming old-fashioned; would concoct opinions derived from images conveyed by television presentation. Secularisation of the constitution, carried out as a formal constitutional provision, would replace Christianity with the unstated Humanism that is prevalent within the intelligentsia. It is Humanism expressed in a very imprecise fashion, precisely because it is largely undefined. Its lack of a theoretical rendition doubtlessly corresponds with the English *penchant* for pragmatism, and the new assemblage of anomalies and constitutional inconsistencies which would succeed the Disestablishment of the Christian religion would probably be sympathetically acclaimed by a substantial section of the Church's own leadership, forever anxious to ingratiate itself with prevalent liberal opinion. But the gain is unclear. Normally in human social development one set of sacral beliefs is only ditched when another, with a coherent representation, is to hand – or is imposed by conquest. In the present situation in England secularisation is probably the preferred course of only a small minority. The internal secularisation of the Church, however, is likely to produce a situation in which it is their voice, rather than the inarticulate murmurings of the demos, which is likely to prevail.

14

Community

The Church is the body of Christ in the world. This is nearly a literal description for those who locate themselves in the tradition of the historic understanding of Christianity: Christ committed himself to a living company of people, who were for all time to convey his truth. To be a Christian is to be integrated with this body, this company; to be separated from it is to lose not only the organic vitality of a universal society but also the authority to witness to orthodox belief. The Church may be said to be a 'community' in a specialised sense, therefore. It is a community which exists both in time and in eternity and whose sole purpose is to be Christ in action – it has no other function than demonstrating and transmitting his truth. Those who are called to this body are therefore members of a community whose purposes are set by an absolute sovereign; their ideas about reality are intended to conform precisely to the message proclaimed in the life of Christ when he was corporeally in the world. They have no independence, and are not allowed what modern society has come to expect as a species of personal entitlement – the right to determine sacral values for themselves. Christians are people under discipline (another difficult concept for those who exist in a popular culture of libertarianism), whose vocation is to behave as Christ wills. They are also mere mortals, however, and both their understanding and their actions are corrupted by their humanity. Yet as members of an eternal community they are able to draw upon a resource greater than themselves as individuals; they are, that is to say, incomplete until they find their unity in the creator of all things. The 'community of believers' is a real expression: it announces the existence of Christ everywhere, in every dimension of the creation that men and women can see and know about, and in the unknowable fullness of the divine purposes.

Now it also happens that the concept of 'community' has become a buzz-word of the socially enlightened and politically correct. It has become one of the great orthodoxies of the day, and is virtually unquestioned. 'Re-building community' is the aspiration of reformers, the piety of social engineers. But what does it mean? There is an immediate paradox: community by definition means conformity to defined social and moral norms or sacral values, yet modern people exist in a highly individualistic culture in which they expect to exercise personal choice in the values they espouse. Community in traditional society actually broke up because men and women left the social thrall of the rural communities – and the domination of the parson and the squire – to seek personal freedom, as well as the prospect of increased earnings, in the new urban centres. That was at the end of the eighteenth century, and through the nineteenth; the process may still be seen at work throughout the Developing World, however. Modern people are indeed notable for their rejection of conformity to prescribed authority, both in ideas and in the manner in which they perceive political society. In reality, of course, they are slavish adherents of all kinds of orthodoxies of opinion and conduct – but it is not what they believe they are doing. The modern person believes himself in large measure autonomous, entitled to individual choice; able, through education, to select values and to practise them with enlightened respect for others but ultimately because they represent personal sanction.

Yet these same people are constantly talking about the desirability of 'community'. They attribute the social and moral evils of the time to the breakdown of community – crime, moral delinquency, social indiscipline, ordinary self-ishness, the vague and pervasive consciousness of *anomie* which hedges modern commentary on the social state. Everyone wants to 'rebuild community' as the essential panacea, the way of restoring a better mode of existing in the social state. The trouble is that the lost order they aspire to restore never existed. The rural idyll actually comprised social misery, unhealthy housing, political injustice and institutionalised deference. The small-town and community-conscious styles of living of the imaginatively reconstructed ideals of modern social romanticism are largely fictions. Community really meant group dictation of individual lives – it was the community who determined what religion a person should adopt, what marriage partner would be selected, what employment a child would be obliged to undertake for life. Community was broken up to get rid of all of that – it was a moment of personal liberation; and modern individualism, whatever its drawbacks, is the result. Does anyone really want to return to genuine community? It is unlikely; society expects the priority of personal choice to expand still further, not to implode to the scale of a traditional village. Indeed there are no examples of traditional community left in England today. Appearances are romanticised deceptions. Universal education, electronic communication (especially television), the computer revolution, the rise of new and artic-ulate social myths, have despatched effective diversity: a single culture, existing in different levels and reflecting the survival of class consciousness, has come to inhabit both rural and urban, the more and the less socially homogenous. Most of those who go on about the virtues of community life in rural areas are themselves recent arrivals from the cities; most of those in the community-less cities who lament the absence of social camaraderie would be appalled if they were really to be subjected to any.

The whole texture of assumptions about the importance of 'community' is woven from insubstantial threads of social myth. The idea that the current ideal of 'caring' is better expressed in self-conscious communities is actually a very questionable one: does it mean the latter-day sentiments of the distantly remembered slums, where people were forever popping next door with a word of cheer and a cup of sugar, or does it mean the disciplined street committees of the Cuban revolution, with their tight ideological control? Transpose paedophile watch for Leninist political correctness, and the street committee is the model of which England has produced some lamentable recent examples. Community conscious-ness, if it proceeds from empty sentiment to structural reality, is merely a device – it is the device which propagates whatever available ideology achieves ascendancy. Who wants to surrender the highly individualistic choices, and the close family units, which at present characterise lifestyles, for communal choice? Those who clamour for the resuscitation of community values, and the rebuilding of actual communities, do not know what they are asking for.

One thing is certain, however, and that is the secularity of the modern concept of community. It represents, in fact, another example of the secularisation of moral value. The idealism and romanticism of the community, in the vision of its would-be revivalists, does not in general incorporate a religious purpose. Their intention is social control, in however sanitised a fashion: it is to lessen social incoherence and increase the provision of welfare. So greatly has the rhetoric of community values become inflated, indeed, that virtually all the perceived miseries of life on earth can seem to be positively addressed and then eliminated by spasms of community consciousness. It is believed that people are nicer to one another when they live 'in community' – a very dubious conclusion, since people would appear to enhance their dislike of others in increased proportion to the extent to which they get to know them. But then current Humanist culture takes an optimistic view of human nature.

Onto the already over-full community bandwagon have come the churches, never able to resist social moralism at its most self-assured. For the Protestant denominations there were already sympathetic resonances in their foundation conviction that the truth of religion is authenticated by the experience of faith among believers. For the historic churches – the Catholics and the Anglicans – there was a ready openness, and then broad acceptance, of the enthusiasm for community expressed widely in social discourse. What then happened is much more problematical. The Anglicans, especially, began to reinvent their mission to the world around the secular understanding of community as popularised by the social moralists. In place of the Church interpreted as a divine teaching office – as a community of the body of the Lord existing simultaneously in time and in eternity – they began to see themselves as an agglomerate of actual earthly communities, whose propagation of the faith was made to depend on the extent to which they expressed the experience of human values of association, service and fellowship. The clergy began to be trained to regard 'building community', both in the secular society of the world and in their use of resources in their parishes, as the priority. Indeed the whole understanding of Christianity was made to be the vehicle of a social vision – the Church as the harbinger of human values, of camaraderie, of organised caring. Doctrine was secondary to this – nothing very novel in Anglicanism in that – and each minister began to be encouraged to cultivate an interpretation of the faith on a personal basis, and to envisage ministry itself as inspiring others in the parish to do the same. Thus the privatising of religious understanding, the dependence of faith on emotional and aesthetic experience, and the interpretation of core Christianity as an application of community service, came together. The result describes Christianity as currently being conveyed by a sizeable majority of its institutional leaders.

Those engaged in furthering this reorientation of the Church's self-identity seem too close to the values they are implementing to recognise just how secularising the effects are going to be. Where they do, they are not alarmed: their efforts, they imagine, are a legitimate, even the only truly authentic, manner of establishing the Kingdom in the world. Here, they contend, is the Gospel in application; human fellowship as the very embodiment of the body of Christ. That the priority of repentance, and of the terrifying and permanent consequences of sin for the spiritual condition of the individual believer, have become rather secondary matters, seems not to worry the modern Church. The concept of sin, in fact, is readily generalised; it is evident in wrong social practices like racism or sexism. Once again the Church and the secular Humanists are in agreement. An understanding of Christianity as quintessentially the 'building of community', however, has a particular hazard when it is applied at a moment in the Church's history, like the present one, when it is in advanced numerical decline. For the little Christian communities, which are to leaven society by their spiritual example, are becoming *so* small that the participating personnel are beginning, in many parishes, to become markedly unrepresentative of society in general. Far from demonstrating that 'building community' is fostering the Kingdom of Christ on earth, the parishes are on the edge of showing that it actually encourages further melt-down. Those who once went to church but have lost the habit – the great company of nominal believers, in fact – should they enter the local church at, perhaps, Christmas or Easter, in a quasi-nostalgic resurgence of faith, will find a tiny company of inbred enthusiasts practising social camaraderie and conducting new services in

which personal participation is *de rigeur.* It is not likely to
appeal. Simulations of human warmth are inevitably pretty
difficult to arrange, and in the circumstances of modern
Western living, characterised by families choosing ever more
private and individualised styles of social being, many church
gatherings must seem initially embarrassing and then
frankly bizarre. Some, determined, still, to find a place where
remembered religion may be provided, resort to the
anonymity and splendour of the great cathedrals.

In the 1970s the cathedrals saw an influx of worshippers,
drawn there by antipathy towards the then liturgical experi-
mentation. Interestingly (or tellingly) it was the conversion of
the symbolical 'kiss of peace' to an actual kiss which put
many off: so much for the appeal of warm human camaraderie. These 1970s infusions have run their course; the new
congregations then acquired by the cathedrals are beginning
to die off. The invention of *Common Worship* in the Church of
England, however, is likely to see a comparable phenomenon
but on a smaller scale. New worshippers – or, rather, return-
ing worshippers – can be expected to attend cathedral
services on special occasions in the liturgical year; another
wave of refugees. This in turn assists the eccentricity of the
self-conscious 'community' still worshipping in the local
churches as the numbers diminish. With each stage of
numerical decline the chances of appealing to society in
general are lessened. The costs of maintaining the operation
are increasingly difficult to meet. One consequence of recent
reforms of worship in the Anglican Church is that local choice
is now exercised by worship committees: when the numbers
get really low those taking part are no longer adequately
qualified to make any other than quite random choices in
matters which, to the world at large, are the indicators of
what Christianity is all about. Yet the leadership of
the Church persists in regarding the parish as overwhelmingly the paramount unit of the Christian mission, and

increasingly only those with long experience of parish ministry are called to participate in the government of the Church. As a strategy for addressing society it is plainly unsuitable in modern circumstances.

The more the emphasis is on the parish the less the prospect of addressing the world. Eventual financial collapse will probably change the situation, but until then the absence of an effective non-parochial strategy, combined with the conversion of the local congregations into what are in reality closed communities, is not promising. Another sign of the growing sectarian self-identity of the Church – for that is what it is – is seen in the new habit of the leaders associating themselves with the designation 'Faith Communities'. The nation is envisaged as a religious pluralism in which Christianity is one of the components. As a factual description that is true enough. But when the label is owned as a means of locating their own mission, the leaders show a retreat from a vision in which the whole of society is within its pastoral care to one in which each 'community' witnesses to what is judged distinctive in itself.

15

Leadership

The way in which leadership is exercised and understood within the Church has also become in some measure secularised. There is nothing new in the adoption by religious authorities of the styles of organisation and government conventional within the societies in which they are set. The diocesan structure itself is founded upon a Roman civic model, and early church buildings were based not upon the Jewish synagogue but on the Roman basilican hall. The hierarchical nature of Church authority derived from the Byzantine world-picture. The system of patronage common throughout the Latin Church since the early Middle Ages derived from feudal custom. The erastian governance of the Church of England reflected the rise of the nation state and developments in the concept of princely authority characteristic of the sixteenth century. Modern representative institutions in the Church were first essayed in the 13 American colonies following their rebellion against the English Crown, and were based upon the secular institutions of government set up in the emergent independent states. The synodical arrangements now obtaining within Anglicanism echo parliamentary styles. But there is a key difference to be noted in such progressions: the ancient world did not have secular political cultures, and nor did the modern world until comparatively recent times.

The Early Church operated within an historical context

which included alien and pagan religious institutions, not secular ones. And the Christianisation of the Western world resulted in close associations of Church and state, and in numerous attempts to make social and moral culture correspond to what were conceived to be Christian models. Modern secularisation is a novelty, especially since it coincides with the birth of the collectivist state with its extensive powers and its autonomous claims to moral authority. When the Church today borrows from secular modes of organisation and management, it is much more liable to import secular concepts of its own identity than in the past. And that, indeed, is now happening. Practices of accountability, and appraisement of individual priests, for example, though in themselves seemingly desirable both because they may enhance efficiency and also because they allow the world to see that the procedures of the Church are recognisably in tune with what are perceived to be good practice and openness, are nevertheless different in kind from traditional relationships which had expressed bonds of shared communion and love rather than agreed standards of efficient discharge of responsibility. Perhaps this is only a matter of tone and personal disposition: but the Church is *not* like the world, even in the conduct of its institutional operation. It is the body of Christ in the world, and its officers and members, all of whom share the royal priesthood of believers, have a relationship which is intended to simulate eternity.

With modern methods of management, however, have also come modern bureaucratic procedures. The Church, viewed as a bureaucracy, can signal some very alien features. This is not to vilify, for example, the ancient organisational structure of the Catholic Church, centred in Rome, which always attempted, as it still does, to combine holiness and material efficiency – not always, according to its critics, successfully. But it is to remark that modern bureaucracy seems to be peculiarly de-personalising. All bureaucracies have an output of records; it is one of the things which defines them. The modern Church of England shows how subsuming relationships of holiness, and the obligations of service which are not set upon a tariff of worldly achievement, beneath the weight of reports composed by committees and scrutinised by assemblies, does have a distinct tendency to spiritual desensitising. It is a matter of judgement. More conventional reservations, about the over-staffing and excessive costs of bureaucracy, on the other hand, are more easily established. Yet some kind of rationalisation of the organisational structure of any large institution is inevitable and desirable: the question at issue is whether or not the present ones, aping the practices of the world as they do, are more or less liable to assist the internal secularisation of the Church.

Whether the leadership of the Churches, and especially the Church of England, is less gifted or accomplished in the practices of leadership than in the past – and therefore more liable to slide into secular uses through simple unawareness of the implications of their actions – is a matter which is best left unexplored. Let it be noticed, however, that Anglican leadership in, for example, the nineteenth century, despite a high level of positive self-appraisal which has passed uncriticised into the record, might not inspire great confidence. Nor should Winston Churchill's assessment of William Temple be forgotten when he was obliged to prefer him to the Archbishopric of Canterbury: 'the only shilling item in a sixpenny bazaar'. The local leadership of the Church may surely be judged to have suffered – if not declined, at least changed. The educational levels of the clergy, evaluated against a society of increasingly advanced standards, is surely less favourable than it was in the first two-thirds of the twentieth century. Those who believe otherwise point to formal degree qualifications – an assessment without real meaning because the enormous expansion in higher education has in the last two decades altered the relative values which have to be accorded to degree status. It is also true that a majority of the clergy now being admitted to the ministry have already followed a preceding professional career, and are possessed of qualifications appropriate to it. Yet however many variants are introduced to the calculation, commonsense observation indicates the existence of a less educated clergy in a society of increased educational sophistication.

There is no reason to suppose that reduced educational accomplishment makes the clergy more liable to succumb to secularised understandings of their faith, or more likely to adopt secular practices: indeed, in a secularised intellectual culture like the prevalent one there is something to be said for the conclusion that the less acquainted with its leading assumptions they are, the greater the possibility that they may retain some sense of authentic spirituality. But a less educationally gifted body of teachers of the faith is not going to attract the respect of the educated élites who set the terms of reference within which modern public life operates. And this is also at a time when the Church, as an institution, has less and less access to public debate. It has already effectively lost any structured means of addressing social, moral or political culture. Its voice is heard, where it is heard at all, as one among many – baying at the gates of the citadel of public virtue along with all the other interest groups, voluntary societies and ex-pundits. The clergy, unhappily, is becoming deeply demoralised as a professional category; their spiritual disorientation corresponds in some measure to the seeping away of their former social rôle and identity. Only the Evangelical ministers, who anyway derive from a tradition of Protestant Christianity which always demonstrated distinctly sectarian qualities, seem untouched by the malaise of the times. And as a terrifying backdrop to what no one will openly admit is an institutional and vocational crisis, is the continuing reduction of attendances at church.

The senior leaders of the Church are either unaware of the

true nature of the decline or choose not to dwell upon it; they are increasingly preoccupied by internal issues prompted by bureaucratic requirements – as are most professional leaders at the present time. They are constantly in receipt of over-optimistic accounts of their stewardship represented to them by the clergy, who are in effect manoeuvred into such near-falsehoods by the need to give evidence of activity urged on them by the appraisal system. Isolated by the geographical dictates of the parochial system; educationally ill-equipped to avail themselves of detached prophetic discernment; and dis-illusioned at the poor results of the ministerial experiments set up with bewildering frequency by consultative bodies who never really seem to consult anybody: the clergy are remark-able for the quiet heroism with which they recognise their fate. At all levels of leadership there is an unhealthy indul-gence of ambition, an unnecessary attention to minor in-house issues, an endless and presumably groundless belief that ceaseless choice and change will prompt regeneration. By most of the tests that a social scientist might apply to evaluate the decline of an institution, the Church in modern England shows a high level of failure. Nothing in the life of the nation should sadden the observer more. But a de-moralised leadership, as the clergy now appear to be, is the saddest feature of all. It does not help when the senior leaders seem impervious to recognition of the evidences before them.

There is one particular characteristic of the Anglican lead-ership, of long standing and with affinities to the behaviour of influential figures in secular society, which helps to account for aspects of their receding effectiveness. This is their horror of controversy. It is much approved in English public life that pragmatic solutions to divisive problems should be sought out and implemented. The result is the supposedly states-manlike middle-ground formulae, the 'commonsense' accommodations of difference, the forms of words which

appear to bridge gulfs. These may prove useful in the arts of
government in boardroom wrangles; in the governance of the
body of Christ, however, which is all about the preservation of
truth, and its representation with clarity in the cultural
expressions of each age and society, fudges (to use the precise
word) are highly inappropriate. The bishops cannot resist
them. With a vision which sometimes does not extend beyond
their own retiring age, and with a disinclination to make
their hands sticky with the blood of controversy, the leaders
of the Church rarely address the really important questions
since these are the ones which are inevitably divisive. It is,
however, only in the short term that complicated institutions
are preserved by limited fixes: for long-term survival, people
of long vision need to think in terms of centuries – as the
Vatican has always done, hence the notorious slowness of its
decision-making process. Compromises in the conveyance of
truth, and forms of words which accommodate genuine
differences of interpretation, may appear wise and states-
manlike to the leaders of this generation, but they are not the
way to preserve truth. And the Church has always been full
of division – there was never a golden age of undisputed
unity. In each moment of division the nettle has to be
grasped, the truth maintained, and an acceptance that those
who dissent will depart not in peace but in schism. The
history of the Church is a history of controversy. It may be
said, indeed, that the existence of controversy is an indication
of vitality. All the great systems of belief and applied ideologies, including the Church of Christ and, for example,
Marxism, have been characterised by differences of opinion,
the production of heresies, and the formation of splinter
groups – some of them, in fact, both large and of long
duration. Anglicanism, for example, has so far lasted about
the same length of time as the early Donatist heresy (in
which, incidentally, the laity remained faithful and it was the
bishops who were heretical). It is to be hoped that longevity,

however, is the only characteristic which Anglicanism holds in common with the Donatists. Difference of opinion, the testing of propositions of interpretation, the permanent re-definition of orthodoxy and its opponents: these are the marks of a truly living institution, a sign that the organic being is living in the real world of ideological conflict. The Anglican horror of controversy tends to disqualify the Church from participation in the everlasting process by which truth is refreshed. Then there is a kind of stasis; in the increasingly stagnant waters the living creatures move in ever murkier light and feed off the sickly and prolific growths. In another and more popular verbal image, the Anglicans believe they are a 'branch' of historic Catholic Christendom. If this is so, their dislike of taking part in the attrition of ideas – in the means of maintaining the evidences of vitality – implies that they are slender offshoots of the parent plant indeed.

There are practical results of the leaders' antipathy to controversy, of their rush to espouse compromise solutions to every ideological difficulty. Chief of these, in modern times, has been the practical and undeclared schism over the question (now the practice) of ordaining women to the historic priesthood. There is an extraordinary resulting inconsistency. In 1996, in the terms of the Porvoo Declaration, the Nordic Lutheran and the British and Irish Anglican Churches united. But the Church of England had just voted to ordain women and, faced with substantial division over the matter, arranged to set up a parallel corps of bishops to look after the dissentients and to regularise the existence of parishes which declined to accept the priestly ministry of women. At the time, the successful majority party doubtless calculated that the minority would quite shortly recognise their error and would, anyway, in due course pass away. In fact the Church has, in the following ten years, remained in a steady state of division. The astonishing consequence is that the Church of England is now in communion with the Scandinavian Lutherans but not with itself. A Church led by those who were more prepared to recognise the divisive effects of the necessary work of permanent ideological clarification could not have got itself into this state. Its leaders might have placed truth ahead of attempted compromise. Their problems are going to stack up if this sort of conduct of the Church's affairs persists. For this is an age, especially, when the doctrines, teachings and practices of the Church are going to need progressively more radical re-statement, in circumstances of disintegrating and re-formulating culture. The secular arts of compromise may win a vote in a committee, but they are not calculated to preserve truth in the midst of an ideological hurricane.

16

Priesthood

The various evidences of the internal secularisation of the Church are in themselves serious enough. But institutions, and traditions of thinking, survive by training those who are to transmit their knowledge and distinctive characteristics. Probably the most serious crisis now confronting the Church of England – and only inadequately perceived in the extent of its gravity by the leadership – is its failure to make provision for a sound preparation of its future officers. This is true in relation to both priestly and lay vocational training.

Among the obligations of priesthood the sacrificial are by far the most important – and the most difficult to fulfil. The whole Church is the body of Christ in the world, and the priest as the local representative of that body, and therefore of Christ, has the primary duty to serve Christ before all others. That means, in practice, the priority of ministry above the relationships of the family and of society, and the discipline of teaching what Christ teaches rather than the often alluring values of the encompassing culture. The judgement of the priest in determining what actually is the teaching of Christ, and what is drawn from the accidental intellectual or moral contingencies of society, is not personal: it is determined collectively by the People of God and conveyed through ecclesiastical authority. In the vows of ordination, therefore, the priest eschews private inclinations and the determination of Christian truth by subjective preference and undertakes to teach the objective truths determined by the Church – and no others, at least when it is the authority of priesthood which is being exercised. In a society which esteems individual judgement, and encourages each person to cultivate personalised moral positions in relation to conduct and public affairs, this can be an exceedingly difficult restriction on the intellectual faculties. But it is absolutely fundamental to the calling of priesthood. The sacred ministry is the declaration of Christ to the world: it is *his* word, and not the individual's, which is to be heard. It is sophistry to imagine that the mind of Christ is known by examination of individual experience, or that Christ's will is represented to people in different ways according to the characteristics of their personalities or to their differing spiritual psychologies. Christ is one, and his will is undivided. Despite much modern rhetoric to the contrary, the mind of Christ is not 'discovered' in individual circumstance – although his will for each person may well be *applied* in ways which differ according to circumstance, both of place and of personal temperament. The duty of priesthood – again in contrast to much modern declamation – is not defined through the expression of the interior preferences and emotional luxuriance of individuals but, on the contrary, through the suppression of personal inclinations. It is an emptying out of the personal will in order that the divine will may achieve priority. This does not desiccate the individual person, for if the promises of Christ are truth, as the priest is witness, the profession of Christ itself supplies a new interior richness which is all-sufficient.

The teaching office of priesthood is at the very centre of the vocation: Christ himself sent out his followers to *teach* the people, and the truths which he declared were exclusive. As sacred employees priests operate solely within the teaching sanctioned by those who employ them. To some this will seem extraordinarily illiberal. In fact, however, it is merely what any organisation demands as a matter of common loyalty or ideological rectitude. Who can imagine a political party allowing its members to decide the content of its programme without reference to a general body? No one is allowed to determine the moral value of attitudes to, for example, racial issues or sexual equality: those sacral values are regarded, in modern society, as necessarily regulated by law. And yet within the Church there is a widespread inclination to suppose that priests can evaluate the nature of Christian teaching by private judgement and offer the resulting explanation as a satisfactory presentation of the Christian faith. Indeed, much of the training for ministry of all sorts within the Church of England is currently conducted in an atmosphere of personal experience and selection, so that what eventually emerges as 'Christian' teaching is in reality little more than the opinion of individuals.

The discipline of priesthood begins with the acceptance of authority. Furthermore, authority, for its part, has the duty – which it often presently ignores – of prescribing clearly the nature of the teaching that is required. Courses of study should be stable and uniform throughout the Church, the curriculae in use should be precise and not open-ended, and the students should be conscious that they are being trained to propagate approved interpretations of faith and morals and not their own selections or constructions. This is even more necessary at a time like the present, when the intellectual capacities and educational achievements of those coming forward for ordination are, in relation to the levels general in society, declining. Speculative thought by those who are insufficiently gifted in the attributes of learning will inevitably produce corrosive effects; it will tend, in time, to bring the whole presentation of the Christian religion into intellectual disrepute. Available evidence would seem to prompt the possibility that Christian learning should be recognised, in existing circumstances, as a matter largely for the laity. In view of the past record of distinguished clerical scholarship, and of great institutions of learning formerly under the immediate patronage of the Church, this is a regrettable conclusion. But it is realistic. And in the end it does not matter whether the torch-bearers of Christian learning are clerical or lay – provided the vocation is fulfilled by some well-defined and well-supported group in the Church. The vocation of lay theologians was always recognised as one of authenticity and importance in preceding epochs of church history; more or less exclusive clericalisation of the profession of theology has served the Church well in recent centuries, but is plainly questionable in view of the impending intellectual qualifications of the Anglican clergy. The reality is the laicisation – as well as the secularisation – of modern departments of theology (where they exist) in British institutions of higher education.

The emphasis on so many current courses of ministerial training on the individual perceptions of the students themselves actually indicates an understanding of Christianity which ought to be less readily accepted at face value than it is. For here is the manifestation of a spiritual culture which regards religion itself as primarily derived from emotional need and conveyed through an exercise of the emotions. It is personal experience, in this perception of things, which determines the reception of religious truth – rather than conformity to the traditional teaching of ecclesiastical authority. Religious faith is accordingly rendered as a matter of sentiment, and training for the ministerial vocation easily transforms itself into a collective exploration of shared religious experience. Religious understanding which rests upon the satisfaction of individual emotional requirement, and whose authority resides in personal interpretation of scriptural texts, together with the simple conflation of Christian morality with the transient enthusiasms for humanity which visit every age, has not only a highly relative base but is, in itself, a misconstruing of dogmatic truth. God's will is because it is: not because we believe we experience a need for it. The teaching of Christ is proclaimed not because it has beautiful resonances or gives meaning to individual sensibilities, but because it is true in itself; it does not require group sessions for self-discovery to grasp doctrines which were known to the ancients, are true in all circumstances, and should form the permanent basis of all training for the sacred ministry. It may go strenuously against the grain of the present moment of religious understanding, both inside and outside the Church, but the guiding principle of preparation for ordination should be the acquisition of a known body of Christian teaching, in order to transmit it faithfully; and not a process of self-discovery in the course of which merely human sensation will direct priorities and substances. Priests are not called upon to determine the veracity of the doctrines upheld by the Church, but to teach them.

Nevertheless, accepting the reality of modern scepticism with received values, the existence of an educated society which is encouraged to consider it is capable of independent thought, and the prevalent loss of confidence within the Church's own membership in traditional formulations of the faith, it is plainly desirable that the clergy should be trained to consider the type of queries about Christianity which they will encounter in their ministry. If this is done by creating an atmosphere in which priests themselves are expected to reformulate faith and morals, an enormous range of hazards can be anticipated. In its crudest experience the result will be individual priests defining Christian truth as they go along – a phenomenon already quite familiar and encouraged, indeed, by those who have abandoned the concept of a dogmatic basis to truth. The Church has in fact always included instruction on the manner in which sceptical or hostile questioning of the faith may best be answered, and there remains an impressive number of published works on the matter from preceding centuries. Most of these are arguably unsuited to modern usage, yet the purpose for which they were written remains unaltered. Some recent attempts to furnish modern versions have merely compounded the problem by offering accounts of Christian teaching which are themselves so indebted to scepticism over essentials that they are counter-productive.

It is best to go back to fundamentals: if the priests are trained in a clear understanding of authoritative doctrine the explanations they offer to a questioning culture will carry the authority of a universal institution. It can stand on its own; it does not require re-formulation by individuals. The Church is the body of Christ in the world: by definition, it cannot speak with more than one voice in its presentation of essential doctrines, and priests should be trained accordingly. This understanding, both of the vocation of priesthood and of the nature of ecclesiastical authority, is hugely at variance with a great deal of modern practice in the Church of England.

Personal discipline in the lives of priests is also a matter which is inseparable from the ethos desirable in training. In the manner of private lifestyle, no less than in adhesion to authoritative teaching, a priest is a person under discipline. Avoidance of conduct or moral irregularity which can cause scandal is obvious – though not so easily categorised in a society whose acceptance of behaviour, and especially of sexual behaviour, is in some matters undergoing quite radical transition. These are strangely contrasting times. Increased tolerance to all kinds of heterosexual conduct which would once have been regarded as utterly unacceptable has to be balanced against a sharp new Puritanism which is censorious of conduct in other areas. To this difficult subject the Church brings some fixed rules of conduct to be expected of its own members – but also, as ever in the past, an openness to accommodate legitimate developments in human understanding. It is up to regular institutions of ecclesiastical authority to determine policy in relation to such matters,

and not to assume that the passage of resolutions in ambigu-
ous forms of words can determine issues over which there are
serious differences of substance.

More basic, however, in relation to disciplined living is the
question of loyalty. A priest is called to obedience to Christ
above all other loyalties – including those to family and
friends. It was always argued by those at the time of the
English Reformation, that the marriage of the clergy could
well interpose domestic loyalties which might tempt the
weak to wrong priorities in ministry. The rule of clerical
celibacy, after all, did not derive from negative views about
human sexuality, but from the supposition that a married
clergy would unavoidably put the interests of their wives and
children before their sacred calling. In an age like our own,
with Humanist cultural and moral values, there is a widespread disposition to see no necessary conflict of interests: an
understanding of the Christian faith which emphasises its
human, 'caring', ethicist, and 'relationships' dimensions – so
to say – actually identifies family life, with all its tensions
and conflicts of loyalty, as an important means of applying
Christian teaching and precept. So be it. But as a matter of
fact priests *do* increasingly experience grave difficulty in
putting the exclusive demands of their vocation above the
human issues of personal relationships, and this is exacer-
bated by the ties of family life. Bishops will testify to the
modern growth of marital problems which they encounter
among the clergy. These observations are not intended as a
polemic against a married clergy, nor an encouragement to
celibacy. They are intended neutrally; it is a matter of note
that the training of the clergy should recognise that there are
some loyalties to the Church – as owed therefore to Christ –
which in all circumstances transcend family obligations.

It might once have been added that modest lifestyles
should accompany this, as an incentive to loyalty to calling.
But the truth is that the clergy today are relatively poor as a

profession, and the possibility that an unfavourable contrast may exist between their manner of living and that of the people they are called to serve is unlikely – as once it often did, when, in a class society, the Anglican clergy identified with the more wealthy sections. Yet it is also impossible to escape the impression that the clergy today are often as immersed in the materialist culture as those around them, in terms of ordinary expectations in living standards and leisure pursuits. Whereas this can be, and frequently is, justified on the grounds that it forms a basis of shared experience with the lay world, and so assists the practicalities of ministry, it is also, indisputably, a consequence of relative poverty rather than positive vocational choice. The Church of England probably has much to learn from the Roman Catholics about utilising poverty in material amenities in the disciplined approach to austerity encouraged in the course of training. Anglicanism has often been characterised by a gentle worldliness: present circumstances provide a welcome occasion to make virtue of necessity and to foster simplicity of living as a desired end in itself. The Lord sent out his first followers, after all, with neither purse nor scrip.

A disciplined approach to ordination training includes not only the acceptance of the authority of the Church in general in the teaching actually given, but also obedience to particular ecclesiastical authority. A priest is a person under direct authority. The vows of ordination preclude personal choice, except to the extent that it is conventional in Church practice, in many areas of vocation. There are no circumstances in which a priest – who is a servant of Christ, and therefore of his body in the world – should regard the instructions of his bishop as legitimately subject to personal scrutiny. This is a discipline, too, which will at once appear to be at great variance with the current practice of the world: today it is usually contended that the individual is possessed of *rights* which transcend conventional authority. It is today, indeed, *automatic* adhesion to authority – as in atrocities committed in situations of conflict – which is demonised, and the hero of the modern moral sense is the person who questions his orders and disobeys them in fulfilment of the intimations of conscience. Such a tableau is not applicable to the exercise of authority in the Church, and priests are called upon to practise obedience in all circumstances, even when their personal judgement indicates principled opposition. The atmosphere of training should from the start cultivate a disposition to assent: it is Christ who is being obeyed, not the mere agent on earth who conveys what he believes to be the divine will, and may well make mistakes in the process. The practice of the Church of England has nearly always allowed for reasoned exchange of views about vocational decisions; obedience, when a decision is made, ought to be regarded as obligatory. This is all the more taxing, and in consequence will evoke the greater nobility of calling, when assent has to be made to decisions from which the individual may wish to dissent.

There is some difference, yet again, between modern approval of emotional involvement in situations of pastoral care and a more detached professionalism of the sort once regarded as desirable. People today esteem passionate commitment, even in such work as journalism – which was once judged the more effective for being as distant as possible from personal involvement in the issues being reported. An experienced priest will have seen the pastoral matters that arise many times before, and training should consciously and deliberately prepare for the assembly of a body of expertise rather than a set of emotional responses. In the great scale of things the searing disasters that afflict individuals or families are relatively insignificant. It is one of the glories of the Christian religion that it is about a God who *is* involved in individual lives – but it is God who is involved, not the priest. Priestly ministry is an agency; it requires judgement, detachment and balance of assessment. Pastoral advice is best when it is realistic: it may not be what the recipient wants to hear. This is not the emollient office of universal and indiscriminate niceness, but God's dealings with the world rendered in the fallible capabilities of his earthly representatives. Christ declared that sins would be retained as well as forgiven by his ministers, and to be of real service the priestly ministry must sometimes involve censure as well as consolation. Personal detachment is essential in a priest; if human passions are allowed to engage with situations of human dislocation the result will be earthly, and not heavenly, advice.

Priests should also be trained to be cautious about joining associations, parties and pressure groups seeking seemingly righteous or beneficial ends. For they bring with their adhesion the authority of God, however much they attempt to make their involvement personal; and collective action, by its very nature, holds out the prospect of divisiveness, and the opportunity for the infiltration of ostensibly good causes by all manner of opportunists and those with ulterior purposes. Priests are in the service of the greatest of all collective organisations – the Church of Christ – and do not need to resort to other associations in order to secure the purposes of the Kingdom.

17

Ministry

There would appear to be considerable indecisiveness, particularly within local Anglican bodies, about the distinction between lay and clerical ministry. In discussing such issues as lay celebration of the Eucharist, for example, attempts characterised by descending levels of sophistication are made to determine what is authentically distinctive about priestly function. There should, however, be no ambiguity. The question is not really one of leadership but of identity. All the followers of Christ constitute a priesthood, but Christ himself designated a particular group who were to convey his message of salvation to the world, and whom he explicitly sent out, in his name, as his representatives: the 70 and the apostles. They were commissioned to celebrate the great final supper of the Lord ('Do this in remembrance of me') and to administer his authority ('whose sins you forgive, they are forgiven'). Subsequently identified with the priestly line of Melchizedech, those given authority in the Church were regarded as separated from the general body of the believers, not by virtue of special insights or prophetic gifts, nor by proven abilities of leadership or skills in teaching, but by being the immediate representatives of Christ. They were given, that is to say, authority. It is Christ who presides at the Eucharist, and Christ who forgives sins: his human agent belongs to a distinctive order to effect the union of the seen and the unseen worlds. As the substitute of God himself for

those specific purposes, it is only right that priesthood should
imply a measure of separation from the world, and that those
called to it should be recognised, in the dignity of their
calling, as possessed of clear identity. It is also true, at the
ordinary human level, that all institutions require a recognisable structure, held together by authoritative rules of
membership, and visible to the discernment of the generality.
But there is no reason why priests should necessarily constitute a monopoly – or even a majority – in such a structure,
since within Christianity the royal priesthood of Christ
inhabits all who are loyal to him. In the religions of Greece
the *hiereus* had a special relationship to the gods, but often
operated within a structure of observances which was determined by civic authorities: in Rome, similarly, the *sacerdos*
had special access to the divinities yet was not in any effective sense their organisational agent. The Church of Christ
subsists in all his baptised followers: they are exclusively his
body in the world.

Many of those enquiring about the distinction between the
lay and the ordained ministry have resorted to Christian
origins. This is not as helpful as it might seem. Christianity
was intended to be, and is, teleological: the image used by
Christ himself was of the mustard seed. It is not particularly
instructive to evaluate the authenticity of any body or ideal
by reference to its original condition: democracy has grown
out of feudalism but bears no resemblance to it: the Christian
Church has grown out of what could well have been a resurrection cult. It is no significance. What matters is the
development: how change and dialectical exchange with the
surrounding culture has produced the visible Church. Its
treasures are both new and old. So with priesthood: the body
of Christ in the world is defined according to the understanding of those who are its agents at any moment of time. It is
therefore absolutely essential – in a condition of permanent
flux – that there should be an institutionalised means of

determining what is a legitimate development and what is a corruption. Authority is needed not only to advance truth but to identify error. In Christianity that authority resides in the whole People of God, and it is deployed through the structure, priestly and lay, which has evolved. Authority and structure alike are most usefully evaluated by reference to their performance in existing conditions, rather than by reference back to primitive models. In fact, as it happens, there has been a remarkable consistency of development in Christian history – taking a broad view. Although the whole Church is the repository of the authority of Christ, however, the institutional structure necessarily embodies – literally – the will of Christ. And here priesthood may be seen to represent Christ in the mysteries of his central act of expiation: in the sacramental presence of the altar and in the forgiveness of sin. But *all* Christians are called to teach his truth, to minister to the sick and to console the distressed, to participate in such management as may be required to perpetuate the faith, and to be Christ for the world to see.

The qualities of 'leadership' are often referred to when the gifts of the lay ministry are essayed. This, however, can be an opaque reference, since in secular usage leadership can involve practices scarcely appropriate in the vocational ties of ministry. A minister of Christ, whether clerical or lay, has obligations which transcend management and may properly be described in quasi-sacramental language. 'Authority' in the Church is about the authenticity of the faith; 'leadership' is about the exercise of discipline in the Church by those who are servants. What is looked for in the ministers of Christ, clerical or lay, is wisdom and sound judgement rather than the potential to operate in an executive capacity. It is arguably a significant incentive to the internal secularisation which has characterised some aspects of modern ecclesiastical experience that models of authority appropriate to control and management in worldly professional life have been too uncritically imported. It is also probably true that in a normal parish the leadership potential of many lay people will equal that of the ministers, but since all are co-operating in a voluntary society, the kind of sanctions available to help preserve discipline in the secular world are not suitable or desirable. Leadership, as a consequence, has to be exercised in a very specialist sense, and it is much more likely that wise judgement will command an effective response among Christian congregations and in Christian organisations than will, for example, the conventional deployment of management skills. These observations are not intended to apply to ordinary efficiency or to planned action – which are assumed to be required in ministers of all sorts – but to the manner in which spiritual priorities are given institutional expression. Lay ministry is essentially about the creation of the Kingdom of Christ; those are called to it whose vocational sense is as intense as those called to the ordained ministry. It is, however, different in kind. In virtually all the classic religions the great mysteries disclosed to the initiates are protected by a priestly company solely dedicated for the purpose.

It is the teaching office of the laity which most stands in need of special attention at the present time, and where particular emphasis in the course of training is urgently necessary. The Church of England, to put it bleakly, does not make adequate provision for the teaching of Christianity. It has in recent times made no serious effort at Christian education in a confessional sense: there is no effective institution dedicated to the intellectual advancement of Christianity. The Anglicans live on borrowed time, assuming that the liberal education which they sponsor through their presence in schools and colleges will somehow suffice. It simply will not. But the parishes, and the resources of some of the cathedrals, do still offer the chance of taking education in Christianity seriously. First, however, the clerical and lay ministers – and especially the lay ministers – need to have an educational function much more consciously built into their training. Since it is the laity, rather than the clergy, who in existing circumstances are likely to be the more educated part of the ministry, considered as a whole, it is the laity who should take the initiative here. This is not intended to suggest a further multiplication of all those barren group discussions about 'Christian values' or current issues to which Christianity might address itself, which seem to form the present staple of Christian teaching in the parishes and cathedrals, but actual instruction of the people in Christian doctrine, morality and history. No body of ideas can survive if it does not make its future propagation a matter of supreme urgency. And it does not help to present such ideas as open-ended probabilities, or to attach them to a culture of scepticism and intellectual relativism. Christianity needs to be taught in the parishes solely because it is in itself true.

It is therefore crucial that the teachers should themselves be taught, and that Christian essentials should be taught as certainties. Many of the laity seeking ministerial training are themselves members of professions which have a strong educational dimension. This can be of enormous value to the Church. At the same time, however, by allowing modes of thought and cultural references appropriate in the secular world to become the method employed in sacred learning, there could well be an unconscious secularisation of the faith unless the gifts of the laity are very specifically designated. Teaching the doctrine of Justification by Faith, for example, may well be ineffectual if the methods used, and the intellectual references cited, are only those appropriate to liberal arts courses in an institution of higher education. It is also true that those giving the teaching must be explicit Christian believers. This will seem an odd thing to add; but it is astonishing to discover how often it is regarded as perfectly acceptable for educational expertise to be considered preferable to commitment to faith in the current procedures for the selection of staff in – let us say – an Anglican college of education, or a church secondary school. Lay (or clerical) teaching of Christian truth should not primarily be an exploration of all available viewpoints, or considered an exercise in open discussion, but an unambiguously committed presentation. It is of course valuable, in order that individuals may defend this faith (both because of their own possible interior reservations and because of intellectual assault by others), that arguments against Christian faith and morals are included in the training of ministers and in the courses they give. At no costs, however, should the main body of ministerial teaching of Christianity represent it as one among a number of equally valid systems, or as a series of intellectual propositions awaiting individual assent. Those who come to the Church for an explanation of Christianity should be able to receive a clear and unequivocal statement of it.

The pastoral work of lay ministry is no different in nature from that of the clergy, and the training appropriate for it can be in all essentials identical. It would seem that the pastoral ministry of the clergy has always been much more confidently performed than the spiritual, and there exists, therefore, a considerable body of expertise and experience from which the laity may draw guidance. But it has, over the years, become progressively secularised as the clergy, in their training and in the execution of their tasks, have tended to consider themselves a dimension of welfare services in general. The rise of the 'caring culture' in modern society, and the increasing collectivism of social concern – with its attendant professionalism – have had two effects which are not entirely satisfactory from the point of view of Christian service. The first is to have reduced the area of social work which once was the more or less exclusive preserve of the Church. The second is to have made such social work as is carried out by the Church appear ever more amateur. The second can readily be corrected by better training – and is anyway sometimes self-correcting because so many of those now entering both ordained and lay ministry have had preceding careers in, or are still engaged in, professions which have a strong pastoral or social service element.

Therein lies another problem. The more the pastoral ministry of the Church is professionalised, in accordance with general usage in the modern world, the less evident its distinctly spiritual intention sometimes becomes. No one wills this: it is an almost unavoidable consequence of the present ordering of society. Recent times have witnessed the secularisation of the moral sense, and children in schools are no longer taught to regard moral welfare as related to religion. Christian work in this area needs to be distinctive and unashamedly declared to be inspired by religious conviction. Would adherents of the Islamic faith fail to emphasise publicly that *their* social works are offered as evidence of religious belief?

There has also been an unnoticed shift in vocational sense. Many of those coming forward for the ministry, both ordained and lay, are now more attracted to the idea of a life dedicated to the material welfare of others than they are to saving souls. In some measure this merely indicates the pervasiveness, even inside the ministry of the Church, of universalism. The prospect of dying without a precise assent to faith, which once filled Christians with genuine terror, scarcely comes into modern consciousness. Ministry is not often conceived in terms of a preparation for eternity; it is more usually now thought of as a matter of sanctifying human relationships and striving for a just social order in the world. The pastoral work of the lay ministry, however, should be as rooted as that of the clergy in the salvific priorities of which Christ himself gave example. In seeking the alleviation of human distress, the ministers of Christ are ministering to Christ. Yet, however much the Kingdom begins in the world, and receives its content from actual situations of earthly social exchange and moral conflict, it remains celestial in nature and is entered by those who confess their allegiance to Christ. Whether lay or ordained, the priority of all Christian ministry is the salvation of souls, of right belief, before the also necessary alleviation of human suffering and the pursuit of social righteousness. There are all kinds of ways in which the two can be shown to be related, or even interdependent: the plain and ordinary meaning of the words of Christ clearly require repentance of personal sin and immediate submission to the sovereignty of God, however, before the mere dislocations of the world can be attended to as the means by which the life of the Kingdom may be expressed and given content. The vocation of ministry is spiritual rather than material in intention.

Personal discipline is no less essential in the lay ministry than it is in the ordained. Anyone representing Christ to the world – and that must mean any Christian – carries the responsibility of living in a manner which honours Christ; those bearing office in the Church should be especially circumspect. There ought first to be discipline in matters of doctrine and religious interpretation: teaching should be related directly to the general mind of the Church and not according to individual preference. In the manner of living there ought never to be the possibility of giving offence through scandal. It may sometimes be, of course, that the public is scandalised by things that ought not to be considered improper – as knowledge in such areas as human sexuality, or public attitude to drugs, for example, changes over time. But even when it is possible to consider courses of action to be in themselves acceptable, they should not be adopted, in advance of opinion, by ministers of Christ. Pioneering moral change may be necessary in some circumstances; there are no circumstances, however, in which Christian ministers are called upon to be the pioneers. It is necessary that homosexual ministers – to exemplify a common situation – should live discreetly in order to avoid giving offence, even though this will involve the sacrifice of part of their humanity as well as possible sacrifice of principle. Disciplined living sometimes results in recognising the existence of popular prejudices which are regrettable but which have real effect in setting the terms of social reference in which the Church has to operate. There can never be sacrifice of doctrine and of truth; but something which touches merely the happiness of individuals should be an early candidate for the fulfilment of a sacrificial ministry. Those, in the same vein, whose lifestyles are conventional are also called upon to make sacrifices in their priorities – between the time allocated to the family and to the requirements of lay ministry. No ministry of Christ is 'part time', even though in the daily economy it is secular employment which necessarily predominates. Ministry through work, and the example given to others in the workplace, involve really hard exercises of self-discipline and permanent vigilance. Christ consecrates the world with his presence, and it is those who are called in his name to declare his truth who are the visible sign of the redemption which he so freely offers.

A great deal has been written by various bodies and individuals in the Church of England about ministerial training during the last half-century. Almost all of it, however, has addressed questions of strategy, funding, the prioritising of resources, the recognition of new conditions in the social environment, and similar matters. Important as these several considerations are, the present crisis can best be addressed by re-emphasising the Sacred Ministry itself and the spiritual formation of the ministers.

The eventual demise of the Anglican theological colleges is to be expected. Noble and important as the contribution of these institutions has been in the past, their departure from the scene is not to be lamented. Originally parodies of the bourgeois educational establishments of later Victorian

England, and comparable, even in architectural features, to the public schools, the surviving examples have in recent decades undergone a marked process of internal secularisation. Although ostensibly still able to furnish intimate association between the acquisition of religious and vocational knowledge and the life of devotional practice, the reality is that they have become liberal arts colleges, scarcely distinguishable from the secular institutions of higher education to whose courses and qualifications they freely resort. In most there is virtually no attempt at fostering the kind of disciplined approach for which institutional living furnishes such favourable circumstances. The age profile of the students, it is true, is older than once it was. The intellectual capabilities of both teachers and taught may arguably be concluded to have suffered a decline – relative to the levels commonly found in higher education. But the main reason for the transformation of the theological colleges into liberal arts institutions is the deliberate liberalisation that has occurred in them at the instigation of their own governing bodies. Since the colleges are not under the direct control of the Church and are, rather arcanely, private trusts, there has been little prospect – and, it has to be said, little will – to arrest their de-sacralising. Many of the courses taken by students are those of nearby secular Departments of Religious Studies in secular universities. The commitment to ecumenism, laudable though that may be for other reasons, has broken the link between ministerial training and specific devotional practice. In many colleges students are actively encouraged to make up their own understanding of religion, without particular reference to the traditions of the Church. Since there are permanent differences of view about those very same traditions of the Church, and since these are embodied in denominational differences, the ecumenical priority in many colleges inhibits clarity of purpose. Yet for all this, the reason why the demise of the colleges is to be anticipated is not their internal evidences of self-destruction: it is because of declining recruitment and rising costs.

As an aside to this, it might be suggested that when the time comes for the individual trusts of the various colleges to be wound up, consideration should be given to the reservation of some of the accruing funds, and one of the properties, for the establishment of an Anglican College of Sacred Learning. What might be envisaged is a small college of priests and qualified laymen, of academic distinction, who should provide what the Church of England now so notably lacks: a resource for higher scholarship, under its own patronage and control, with a clear confessional purpose and centred in a shared devotional life. Not since the secularisation of the universities in the nineteenth century, and the secularisation of faculties and departments of theology in the twentieth, has the Church had a place where distinctly Christian learning can be pursued under ecclesiastical auspices. The result has been the liberalisation, partial secularisation, and definite relativising, of the theological understanding available to the Church. The remaining deans of Chapel and pastoral Chaplains in higher education are not an adequate survival for this purpose. The former are in general less distinguished than once they were, and are anyway often appointed by college authorities more anxious to get a moral tutor on the cheap than they are to make provision for the propagation of Anglicanism; the latter have never been learned men, but are typically short-tenure appointments of younger clergy who are required to take services and socialise in the college bar. Nowhere does there exist an effective resource for the furtherance of a distinctly Anglican contribution to scholarship and learning.

Training for the Anglican ministry is only located in the theological colleges for a minority in these days, however. As the age of those coming forward for the ordained ministry has moved from the early 20s to the middle years of life, and as

those concerned are already established in family life, and
with the styles and expectations (and obligations) acquired in
their first professions, the training appropriate to their condition has prompted the evolution of 'part-time' regional
courses. These are now the most common form of ministerial
preparation. There are local variations but the courses are in
all essentials the same. They too, like the theological colleges,
are 'liberal arts' in tone and intellectual atmosphere, and
they, also, usually have a noticeable ecumenical dimension.
The courses are presented and arranged by regional boards
or councils, and are – if at all – only very loosely under the
control of the bishops. Even more than in the colleges,
students are here encouraged to individualise their understanding of Christianity, and to consider this operation of
'self-discovery' an inventive preparation for helping others to
'explore' Christianity for themselves. The entire Christian
religion, indeed, is often represented in terms of personal
experience, with emphasis resting upon shared expressions
of caring, of elevated human relationships and of aesthetic
sensation – this last being regarded as the essence of
worship. (Without intending any kind of polemical observation about the introduction of women to the sacred ministry
in the Church of England, it does have to be noted that the
presentation of religious truth in terms of personal and
emotional experience has been markedly enhanced by it.
There are perhaps enrichments to be gathered here. In
terms of disciplined approaches to the authority of religious
tradition, on the other hand, the results are less encouraging.) It is also noticeable that the approach to academic
theology in the regional courses, as in the colleges, remains
extraordinarily indebted to the modes of thought characteristic of the 1960s. This is quite at variance with the rest of
the world of higher education, where 1960s radicalism has
long been left behind; it appears to indicate a curious *déjà
vu* among the Anglican clergy, whose excited early question-

ings of the Faith seem fixed, as it were, in the aspic of the new courses.

Were it not for these ideological considerations it would be the absence of a sustained residential element in the training courses which most inhibits their potential to provide an adequate preparation for ministry. It is only when the acquisition of knowledge is associated with the liturgical exercises of the Church, in a structured manner, that the disciplines of ministry are most effectively nurtured. For then the honour owed to God in worship is naturally placed alongside the human attempts to understand his will; it is then that the society of the Church is seen to be, not some accessible expression of mere human *camaraderie,* but the sacred company of those sent out by Christ to teach his truth to all nations. Periodic sessions where the trainees arrange themselves in a circle and attempt to discuss momentous ideas which have preoccupied the minds of the greatest thinkers through nearly two thousand years of Christian scholarship are not an adequate substitute for classes which start and end in the spiritual culture of unfolding liturgical practice. Everything has become so informal that the dignity and solemnity of studying the truth of Christ have been lost, and the priceless reservoirs of learning which once supplied the aspirants to Christian service have run into the sands.

18

Decline

Even those who would take the simplest overview of the present nature of English society must surely conclude that it exists with increasingly fewer references to what can be described, in any conventional sense, as religious observance or religious consciousness. There may be all kinds of subtle religious beliefs, substitutes for formal religious structures of ideas, or perhaps unconscious parodies of half-remembered values from a former acquaintance with Christianity. The symbolism of Christian belief remains available for such purposes; and in the physical remains – in the great churches especially – the public, moved as never before by enthusiasm for heritage, encounters a resource which perpetuates, deceptively as it happens, the sense of a national religious presence. The secularisation of the culture is regretted by the public generally, and even by sections of the intelligentsia whose considered apostasy, actually of long standing, is a feature, though not a cause, of the decline of Christianity. That decline derives from such things as the exclusion of time allocated to religious observance by the leisure revolution, from the priorities of vulgar materialism and, above all, from the failure of the Church to address either itself or the public with an adequate understanding of its own message. Decline due to unconscious application of philosophical materialism, the preserve of the intellectuals, has taken a minor part in this, and has only really been important to the extent that applications of their contentions have been filtered through the educational system, the media and the pervasive assumptions of Humanism.

Christianity has not really suffered at the hands of intellectual enlightenment; there has been, indeed, very little inclination to assail it. Its enemy was within, dismantling the walls of the building with all the best intentions and with the zeal of the convert. The Church has been a victim of the adverse cultural conditions in only a limited sense. In another shift of things, the leaders of organised Christianity could well have ridden the storm very adequately: the history of the Church discloses many examples – including the resurgence of Orthodoxy during the centuries that its heartlands were governed by Islamic rulers.

Indeed, the history of the Christian Church shows a kind of providential but elliptical educational process at work – humanity informed by stages of the great truths, and each place and time adding its own enrichment. Again, the parable of the mustard seed points to the developments which have occurred, and which we still see in the evidences of what must otherwise appear to presage universal collapse. The faith has flourished in many cultures and among many peoples. Each dimension of expansion has added new richness to Christian understanding, and from each contraction the wise will learn that spiritual truth is not to be calculated in the currency of earthly expectations. The Lord gives and the Lord takes away. Who now remembers the Christian heartlands of the powerful North African Church of the first five centuries – when the cities of the Nile delta were a second holy land for pilgrims? And what institutional remnants are there of the vibrant faith of Anatolia, or of the great centre of Byzantine spirituality in Constantinople itself? Santa Sophia is a secular museum; where St Paul preached at Ephesus is a hillside of rubble. Like a heavenly dialectic, Christian truth proceeds through human cultures, and there is only the certainty that a decline in the secularised West now will be adjusted by extension in the countries of the Developing World. We are living, in fact, in one of the great ages of Christian expansion. The revival of Orthodoxy, and the enthusiastic reception of the faith in the emergent nations of the southern hemisphere, is shifting the balance of Christianity as the Providential scheme unfolds. Where history has shown decline, it has been due to the chance effects of conquest of peoples by others of alien religious beliefs, or it has been the consequence of radical shifts in population location, or it has accompanied the demise of an entire culture.

What has proved different in modern England, and, as it is turning out, the Western world generally, is the internal secularisation of the Church itself, in its practices, its strategies, in its understanding of the nature of the faith, and – most terrible of all – in its lack of holiness. It has failed to formulate clear alternatives to the traditional teaching it has allowed a section of its leadership to abandon; it is characterised by theological and ecclesiological incoherence. There is an extensive ignorance among Christians themselves about the doctrines of their own faith. The Church has stood by while its supporters have devised understandings of 'Christianity' according to private and individualised selection, unacquainted with religious authority, untouched by considerations beyond the satisfaction of emotional or aesthetic impulses. In the bleak landscape of Christian decline the occasional illumination of particular features of authentic spirituality seems more likely to derive from sources which are outside the institutional leadership; points of direction come from those who have often preserved their knowledge of the faith in spite of, not because of, the measure of sanctity available in what is supposed to be the official treasure-house.

But the Church remains the body of the Lord. Furthermore, precisely because Christianity is completely compatible with modern knowledge, and because there is no sense in which the Western decline is due to a conflict of science and religion, the future of the Church, as it evolves suitable styles for the presentation of its timeless truths in the newly developing areas of the globe, is assured. The saints in heaven must weep, however, to see how the Christians of the West have allowed the secularisation of their own faith to produce such catastrophe. Sustained by false confidence derived from ignorance and failure of sound prophetic insight, and having themselves succumbed to the elevated views of human worth seeping from the earthly ethicism of the times, the Christians of England have probably already lost an adequate perspective from which to appreciate the depth of the crisis around them. So it must have seemed to the last who lit a votive flame in honour of Apollo, or who celebrated as an initiate of Mithras in the ruins of a collapsed empire.

19

Truth

Jesus himself predicted that the numbers of those faithful to him would be small, and that many who identified themselves with his message would prove to be false: 'for many, I say to you, will seek to enter in, and shall not be able;' (Luke 13:24). It is also true that even among the authentic believers there has been an enduring record of disagreement about the nature of the faith, and its application, ever since the beginning. Some have pointed to past social pressures encouraging conformity which have allowed an impression of widespread adhesion to the teachings of the Church, and this must especially have been the case during the many centuries in which the 'Christendom' model of Church and state association received its many and differing embodiments. But the main reason why the size of the true Church of Christ has always been small is the demanding nature of the faith itself. And here is an unlikely paradox. A religion first preached to the rustic people of the lakeside villages of Galilee, and which the Founder declared was to be received with the simplicity of little children, is above all things open to all people. It is precisely because of the nature of people themselves, however, that it is found hard to accept. People prefer a religion of practical help, of ethicised behaviour, of moral exhortation or social engineering – a religion which flatters their sense of self-worth or of the significance of their existence – to a religion which begins, as the message of Jesus begins, with a statement about the intrinsic wretchedness of each person. Modern people do not feel wretched; they have a high estimate of their value.

The religion which Christ came to deliver is about the inability of men and women to put what is wrong with themselves right. It is about human sin, and the flawed nature of each person which renders everyone incapable of self-redemption. Here, as it happens, encased within its very starkness, is the spiritual beauty of Christianity – and the reason why it will endure to the end of time. For Christianity is centred in a phenomenon which is outside of human control: indeed the very attempts now being made, through genetic technology and allied scientific applications, to eliminate the flaws in men and women will only serve to show, in due time, how it is in the nature of humanity to disclose the permanence of essential and ineradicable corruption. Modern Western society seeks a religion of personal elevation, of aesthetic sensation, of social transformation – aspirations which, though represented in the vocabulary and images of 'spirituality' and personal enhancement, are in fact merely worldly. The sanctified earth of their perception suggests the gross pursuit of human happiness – as if God had willed, contrary to the plain record of Scripture, a painless existence for his creatures. Life as a struggle with our baser nature, as an occasion (whose spiritual beauty is made iridescent by its very transience) to transform suffering into the permanence of serving the purpose of God: these characteristics of authentic Christianity do not attract an age which sets welfare and material security as the objects which, it is supposed, describe the real purpose of life on earth. The Church in the Western world is rapidly reinventing itself as the ethicising handmaiden of the aspirations of secular Humanism; it does so by failing to recognise the truth of its own traditional concern with the fallen nature of men and women. The message of Christianity will always exist among those few, in every age, who recognise that the religion of Jesus is addressed, not to the pressing cares of each time and place, but to the inherent imperfections of humanity itself. Many are called to this vocation, but few respond. Charles de Foucauld devoted his life to preaching Christ to the Arabs of the Algerian desert – and in all that time he made no conversions. It is not for us to determine how God judges the earthly issue of the processes of which he is the ultimate author.

The Christian hope is not a better world but personal salvation; the true splendour of the love of God is not that we loved him but that he loved us. To creatures unfitted even for ordered living in the societies of the world he gives immortality: the definitely unworthy receive the treasures of eternity – but only if they attempt each day to recreate lives which embody sorrow for sin. Who now hears conviction of sin resonating from the pulpits of the Church of England? Where now does the aspirant to faith turn who would seek understanding beyond the mere palliation of human inconveniences? The Christian message of the centuries is becoming obscured by modern priorities which relate to only material welfare, which itself is represented as the essence of the faith. First, this produces spiritual barbarity; next, the recession of a religion which when properly understood does not flatter modern humanity's sense of its own entitlement.

Christianity, of course, requires embodiment. Spirituality does not occur in a void, and the social and personal context offers the choice in which its content may receive actual expression. But in our age it is all applications and no religious ideology. And it is becoming an affair of no religious knowledge as well. To serve the needs of others is to serve Christ himself; that, however, is a description of what ought, for Christians, to be commonplace. For it is the external manifestation of an essential and internal re-direction of an individual life. Christian service indicates dedication to God's demands, and is unlike, in intention, the mere performance of social decencies which in every civilised culture has accompanied the ordinary congress of people. Modern people, including many Christian adherents, are now impatient of doctrine – of personal submission to God – and are only too willing to trade it in for the easier allure of the service of humanity. This attracts the plaudits of modern opinion, is less divisive, is now less socially marginalising also, and allows the individual freedom to contrive religious and moral ideas designed to express privately held beliefs.

But God did not will a religion of benign flattery of human values. The Christian hope is precisely derived from the fact that God loves us in spite of what we are. The religion of Jesus will endure because, alone among the religious systems of the world, and elevated not by human estimation and numerical support (but by the man who was God and who died because of our sins) it is a religion which is realistically addressed to our fallen nature. Jesus called people to repentance; that was his priority and it ought to be the priority of the modern Church. And indeed it *is* the priority of the *authentic* modern Church – of those who truly are the body of Christ in the world, loyal to his teaching, wretched in the horrific facts of their humanity, but made spiritually serene by the great love of God. The age has made humanity its god, and far too many who are called as Christians have allowed themselves to accept the human agenda as a reliable embodiment of the message of Christ. So it has actually been in many ages, in reality; for worldliness is a permanent condition. What is peculiar about our age, and our Church in England, is that the general context in which Christian truth is understood has shifted, probably decisively, from the universal and eternal company of all believers to a human consensus about the human worth of men and women. But the traditional understanding of the universality of the Church survives intact: what is Christian truth is what is everywhere and at all times recognised as truth. There is, that is to say, a Church. The body of the Lord is still in the world institutionally, and those whose duty, as members of that body, is to preserve the purity and authenticity of his truth are as faithful as they have ever been. They need to direct their mission to the Christian remnant in England, for there is work to be done.